George Elphinstone Dalrymple

Narrative and reports of the Queensland North East Coast

Expedition

1873

George Elphinstone Dalrymple

Narrative and reports of the Queensland North East Coast Expedition
1873

ISBN/EAN: 9783744646857

Printed in Europe, USA, Canada, Australia, Japan

Cover: Foto ©ninafisch / pixelio.de

More available books at **www.hansebooks.com**

1874.

QUEENSLAND.

NARRATIVE AND REPORTS

OF THE

QUEENSLAND NORTH-EAST COAST EXPEDITION,

1873.

PRESENTED TO BOTH HOUSES OF PARLIAMENT BY COMMAND.

BRISBANE:

BY AUTHORITY: JAMES C. BEAL, GOVERNMENT PRINTER, WILLIAM STREET.

CONTENTS.

			Page
I.—Narrative—Cardwell to Mourilyan Harbor		... ...	5
II.—	„	Mourilyan Harbor and Moresby River	...	8
III.—	„	Glady's Inlet and River Johnstone	9
IV.—	„	Trinity Harbor	15
V.—	„	The Endeavour River ...	19
VI.—	„	Rivers Mulgrave and Russell	23
VII.—	„	Rivers Mossman and Daintree ...	29
VIII.—	„	General Remarks	34
IX.—Appendices A and B			36
X.—Report of Inspector Johnstone, Second in Command			42
XI.—	„	Walter Hill, Esquire, Government Botanist ...	48

Map 1.—Chart of the Coast, New Rivers and Discoveries between Cardwell and Cape Bedford, by
G. Elphinstone Dalrymple, F.R.G.S.   55

REPORTS AND NARRATIVE OF THE NORTH-EAST COAST EXPEDITION, 1873.

Brisbane, 23rd February, 1874.

Sir,

I have the honor to state, for the information of His Excellency the Most Honorable the Marquis of Normanby, in Council, that, pursuant to telegraphic instructions from the Honorable the Colonial Secretary, received at Gilberton on the 1st of September, 1873, I started thence on the 3rd of September, arrived at Cardwell on the 9th, and at once took over from Sub-Inspector Tompson command of the Queensland North-east Coast Expedition, until then in course of organization under his direction.

The objects of that Expedition have been completed in a most satisfactory manner, and I now do myself the honor to hand you report of our proceedings and of discoveries which I believe to be prospectively of great value to this Colony.

The great variety of interesting matter which this exploration has placed in my hands could not possibly be done justice to within the circumscribed limits of an ordinary official report; I have therefore adopted the narrative form, with the object of annexing to it the report of my second in command, Mr. Johnstone, and that of the Botanist, Mr. Hill, with charts and appendices.

The adoption of this form will, I trust, furnish my fellow-colonists with some little information suited to their individual requirements, and will also, I trust, with the able assistance of our Agent-General, enlist British capital and labor in the speedy occupation and development of these new and rich agricultural lands; enquirers being at the same time enabled to form an idea of the scenery, climate, and physical structure of this country of their possible adoption.

I have the honor to offer my apologies for the delay which has taken place in forwarding this Report, having been laid up, ever since my return to Brisbane, with fever caught during the expedition, and a wound caused by a fall from my horse at the Gilbert in August last, and neglected during the voyage, no medicaments of any description having been supplied for the use of the party.

I have the honor to be,

Sir,

Your most obedient Servant,

G. ELPHINSTONE DALRYMPLE.

The Honorable
    The Colonial Secretary,
        &c., &c., &c.

NARRATIVE

On Board the Government Chartered Cutters "Flying Fish" and "Coquette," by G. Elphinstone Dalrymple, F.R.G.S., G.C., P.M., Officer in Charge of the Expedition.

1. Having taken over charge of the Expedition on the 9th of September, I proceeded to inspect the stores and outfit of arms and instruments, etc., forwarded by the Government from Brisbane, and to have the cutter "Flying Fish" properly fitted and prepared for sea.

2. The instructions which I received from the Government were—
   "To explore all rivers, inlets, etc., between Cardwell and the Endeavour River," and
   "1st. To ascertain how far the said rivers are navigable for small craft.
   "2nd. To ascertain the nature of the soil on or near the banks for agricultural purposes.
   "3rd. To assist the Curator in collecting botanical specimens."

3. For prosecuting such labors and carrying an expeditionary party numbering twenty-six men with four months' supplies, the cutter "Flying Fish," of twelve tons, had been chartered, but for so important a service she was evidently quite inadequate.

4. I accordingly telegraphed for, and received permission from the Honorable the Colonial Secretary, to supplement the "Flying Fish" by charter of the cutter "Coquette," of Cardwell, of ten tons, which was accomplished accordingly.

5. Having shipped stores and equipment, we sailed from Cardwell on the 20th of September, and formed our first camp on Gould Island, at the entrance of Rockingham Bay, nine miles from the jetty, there to await return of the "Coquette" from Townsville, complete the organization and discipline of the party, and thence make our final start northwards.

6. On Friday, the 26th September, the cutter "Coquette" joined the Expedition at Gould Island anchorage and took stores, wood, and water on board.

7. We were detained at anchor under Gould Island by a succession of easterly and south-easterly gales from Tuesday, the 23rd, to Monday, the 29th of September, during which time it was not judicious to put to sea with so large a party in such small craft. Had we started, no work could possibly have been performed on a lee shore coast such as that which it was our duty to explore, and which was at the same time obscured by thick weather from all observations.

8. The Expedition was now organised as follows:—
   1st. Officer in Charge, G. Elphinstone Dalrymple.
   2nd. Officer Second in Command, Sub-Inspector F. M. Tompson.
   3rd. Officer in charge of Native Mounted Police, Sub-Inspector R. Johnstone.
   4th. Botanist, Mr. Walter Hill.
   5th. Master (and owner) Cutter "Flying Fish," Mr. Richard Hall.
   6th. Seaman of ditto, Thomas Niell.
   7th. Ditto   ditto, Hugh Niell.
   8th. Master of Cutter "Coquette," C. Nilson.
   9th. Seaman of ditto, Mark Dominico.
   10th. Government Boatman in charge of Police Whaleboat, John Perry.
   11th. Government Boatman, John Vickers.
   12th. Ditto   ditto,   Dod Clarke.
   13th. Cook and Steward, Charles Maidman.
   13 Native Mounted Police Troopers, accustomed to boat work and armed with Snider carbines.
   ———
   Total 26.

The crews were armed with the old smooth-muzzle loaders, the officers and Government boatmen with Westley Richards' double barrel pin-fire carbines. The stores consisted of flour, tea, and sugar, etc., for three and a-half months, and salt and preserved tinned meats for two months, it being intended to supplement the latter with fish and game.

9. The expedition was also supplied with aneroid barometer and thermometers, prismatic compass and field ditto, binoculars, tents with flies, Government blankets for the aborigines, tools, etc., all shipped on board the
   Cutter "Flying Fish," of twelve tons (draft of water 4 feet 6 inches);
   The Cutter "Coquette," of ten tons (draft of water 3 feet 6 inches);
accompanied by the Native Police whaleboat, a dingy furnished by Mr. Sheridan, P.M., Cardwell, and a scow with which to work the mesh net belonging to the master of the first named cutter.

10. On Monday, the 29th of September, the gale abated, and, having exchanged parting cheers with our good friends of Cardwell, who had come out in the schooner "Flirt" to see us off, the cutters "Flying Fish" and "Coquette," attended by the Police whaleboat with crew of black troopers, stood away, N. by W., for Dunk Island anchorage before a fresh south-easterly breeze, with fine weather, showing every island, headland, and inland range clear cut and prominent for observations.

11. The seven small islands of the "Family" Group, steep, and covered with thick woods, were passed on the starboard side. The mouths of the rivers Tully, Murray, Macalister, and Hull showed very distinct broad entrances through the low coast line between Cardwell and Tam O'Shanter Point to port.

12. The low country drained by these rivers, contains much valuable agricultural land, and extends back to the high ranges which are a continuation of the Main Coast Range of Eastern Australia.

13. These mountains are granitic, with occasional interludes of gneiss, quartz, and micaceous schists. Their western slopes, which are drained into the valley of the Upper Herbert from the falls
of

of the Herbert for some sixty miles upwards, are occasionally approached closely by eastern tongues of Leichhardt's great basaltic table land.

14. The lofty range immediately to the rear of Cardwell is a spur of the Main Coast Range—standing out a great mountain buttress towards the ocean—a marked feature of the Australian Eastern Cordillera alluded to in the South by the late Professor J. Beete Jukes,[*] and to be further referred to in this report as repeating itself to the northward.

15. Another great spur, appearing like a separate and independent mountain mass,[†] springs from the Main Range near the heads of the Murray, Macalister, Hull, and Herbert rivers, and runs out on the coast at Tam O'Shanter Point inside Dunk Island, in one summit, reaching the important elevation of 3,965 feet.

16. This great spur, which, like those referred to by Jukes, to the southward, "on the sea-side separates the respective basins of the districts of Gippsland and Twofold Bay, the Shoalhaven River, the Hawkesbury and Hunter Rivers, the Port Macquarie Basin, that of the Clarence River, and that of the district of Moreton Bay," and, we now know, north of the latter divides those of the Mary and Burnett, the Fitzroy, the Pioneer, the Don, the Burdekin, and the Herbert rivers, here again forms the northern boundary of that of the Tully, Murray, Macalister, and Hull, and up to the starting of the expedition, formed the limit of civilization and exploration to the northward.

17. As the richest seaboard lands to the southward are contained within these lateral mountain spurs, so the objects of the expedition were to search for rich tropical lands in the successive basins similarly enclosed to the northward, to survey the estuaries of their drainage, and to determine their capabilities for agriculture, navigation, and commerce.

18. At one p.m. we ran under the western sand-spit of Dunk Island and anchored in three fathoms, muddy bottom, a quarter of a mile from the beach. Camp was formed on shore by Mr. Johnstone, near the watering place of a small creek of beautiful clear water which, coming down out of the hills, enters the eastern and most sheltered corner of the bay, under low cliffs of a sort of sandy conglomerate.

19. Mr. Nind, who was travelling with his own boat and party, in quest of sugar lands, arrived and camped near us.

20. Various parties were detached to explore the island. Mr. Hill collected some interesting botanical specimens and was much pleased with the vegetation and soils.

21. Dunk Island is about nine miles in circumference, and has a back-bone ridge of hills traversing its entire length, rising in the highest part to 860 feet.

22. On their eastern face these hills are rocky and precipitous from the ocean surf line to their summits. The western slopes, however, descend, at first, steep—finally, in more and more gentle descents—to a belt of level ground several hundred yards broad, of very productive looking black sandy loam, suitable for cotton, extending to the sea-side. The step above this, however, and about thirty feet higher, is a broad belt of undulating forest land, richly grassed, of deep chocolate loam, suitable for sugar cultivation. The whole of the hills to their summits have a covering of the same rich deposit. In all about 800 acres of good land, traversed by copious streams of good water, are available on this island; the upper portions for coffee, the middle for sugar, and the coast strip for cotton.

23. Along the margin of the S.W. beach is a belt of magnificent calophyllum trees, the dense masses of their dark laurel-like foliage affording cool and pleasant shade; many fine fig-trees, Eugenias, box, &c., also add to the beauty of this picture of tropical luxuriance of growth and greenery. Some large fig-trees sent out great lateral roots, large as their own trunks, fifty feet into the salt water, an anchor root descending perpendicularly at the extremity to support them. Thence they have sent up another tree as large as the parent stem, at high water presenting the peculiarity of twin trees, on shore and in the sea, connected by a rustic root bridge.

24. The formation of Dunk Island is clay slates and micaceous schist. A level stratum of a soft, greasy, and very red decomposing granitic clay was exposed along the S.W. tide flats, and quartz veins and blue slates were found on the same side of the island further in.

25. Dunk Island is divided from the main land, of which Tam O'Shanter Point forms the picturesque S.E. extremity, by a deep water passage two and a-quarter miles broad, affording a fine entrance and exit from the spacious harbor of Port Hinchinbrook, which is only surpassed on the east coast of Australia by Port Jackson, and is now a place of call of the Torres Straits royal mail steamers.

26. Inside Tam O'Shanter Point is the long sandy beach of Kennedy Bay; a small scrub-shaded creek enters the N.E. corner of the bay, and close to it is a fine young cocoanut tree of about fourteen feet in height, but without fruit. Here, on the 24th of May, 1848, under the guns of H.M.S. "Rattlesnake," the gallant Kennedy landed his party from the "Tam O'Shanter," schooner, to commence that brave though disastrous struggle with the physical features of the York Peninsula, of which there remains but a few chisel-marked camp trees, and the honored memory of the brave leader and some of his followers, who found lonely graves in the cause of exploration.

27. Three members of the party, left by Mr. Kennedy camped near Shelbourne Bay, were never seen or heard of again, and it is possible may have tried to run their tracks back to the southward. At any rate, it is noteworthy that several gins of the Rockingham Bay tribe, now in service in private families and with the native police, are unanimous in their statements that an elderly white man is still resident amongst them, and they associate his capture with "whitefellow leave him wheel-barrow along a 'crab.'" Kennedy abandoned his horse-carts in the scrubs of the Rockingham Bay Range before these gins were born.

28. On Tuesday, the 30th September, camp was struck, all on board by 10:30 a.m., and we stood away for the North Barnard Islands N. ½ E. to clear King Reefs, the black jagged outline of which soon showed above water south of the South Barnard Islands.

29. A narrow passage through and to the west of the main reefs can be used by vessels of light draft of water; but from the number of hidden dangers the use of this inner passage is certainly to be discouraged.

30. From Tam O'Shanter Point to Double Point the coast is bounded by a long sandy beach, from which, as far as Clump Point, a low coast range, parallel to it, rises in densely-wooded slopes. The surrounding

---

* "A Sketch of the Physical Structure of Australia," page 7.   † Ibid.

7

surrounding forest ridges are clothed principally with bloodwood, with good pasturage for cattle. Midway to Clump Point a salt-water creek shows a good opening, but on examination it was found not to be navigable.

31. Several small valleys running back from the coast into that of the Hull River contain a few thousand acres of dense jungle and rich soil suitable for tropical agriculture, their value being enhanced by their close proximity to good pasture lands.

32. Clump Point descends from these coast hills to a rocky bluff to seaward in a long open grassy ridge, dotted with clumps of trees, which gave it a park-like appearance, as we passed it, propelled by a fair S.E. breeze.

33. The South Barnard Islands, consisting of Nos. I. and II. of the group, are high and wooded, their rocky sea faces being, as McGillivray* states, composed "of very thick beds of conglomerate, superimposed upon a compact basaltic-looking rock," rising precipitously from the ocean on the N.E. and S. sides, and falling away on the west to the usual scythe-shaped sand-spit, formed of several raised beaches of broken coral and shells, the most elevated one more or less covered with pumice pebbles and banked up with sand by the meeting of the strong S.E. trades with the southerly set of the flood tides. Such is the character of every high island along this coast, any variation being simply the result of difference in length and the angle of face which they present to the S.E. trades.

34. With the evidence of these raised beaches and pumice pebble deposits at eight to ten feet above the present level of the ocean before one, and with the existence of still more ancient deposits of corals and marine shells on certain portions of the lofty Bunkekin and Clarke table lands, 1,200 to 2,000 feet above the sea, it is difficult to understand how Professor Beete Jukes and Mr. Darwin could have any doubt whatever as to the slow but steady rise from the ocean of Northern as well as Southern Australia, or, according to Mallet's theory, the equally slow and, at times, jerky subsidence of the ocean, to account for these phenomena.

35. These phenomena, and fourteen years of exploration and observation by land and sea in North-eastern Australia, have convinced me that, far from the coral insects having built up a gigantic outwork to the N.E. coast, such as that depicted in Professor Beete Jukes' diagram in the voyage of the "Fly," (vol. I., page 331), that the floor of the ocean is simply a repetition of the descending plateaus which is the formation of the dry land of the Kennedy, Burke, and Cook districts; that the twenty-fathom shore sea, or "inner passage," is but a repetition at a lower level of the up-country table land, whence, as in the precipitous descent of Leichhardt's Range of some three hundred and fifty to four hundred fathoms, it again plunges suddenly down some four hundred fathoms outside the Great Barrier Reefs, which are simply coral structures on the summits of what—were the waters of the Pacific to subside some two thousand seven hundred feet—would be simply another abrupt coast range, descending to another similar seaboard level region, with all its exterior ocean phenomena repeating themselves downwards in successive steps of subsidence to the lowest abyss of volcanic action of the central Pacific basin.

36. Professor Jukes thus graphically describes the contour of the eastern Cordillera of Australia†—"The mountain chain of the eastern coast is, apparently, a rather irregularly formed and complex one, but it seems to preserve the same or very similar features throughout its extent. It is nowhere, so far as is known, a single ridge of mountains, but is made up of many masses of various character—sometimes peaked and serrated ridges; sometimes detached hills, rising from slightly elevated ground; *sometimes great table lands, often ending towards the sea in nearly perpendicular escarpments*; sometimes having on one side or other gentle sloping plains furrowed by innumerable precipitous gulleys and ravines. Large lateral spurs often diverge on either hand from the central portion of the chain, and, especially on its seaward side, appear like separate and independent mountain masses." The description of the Great Barrier and inner reefs and sea in Jukes' "Voyage of H.M.S. 'Fly'" shows a most startling repetition of this formation beneath the ocean; and in the lofty rocky islands and reefs of the inner passage, the same geological formation as that of the mainland. The table-land appearance of the inner passage out to the Great Barrier Reef, with its external "perpendicular escarpment" beyond; and the Atolls, or coral-tipped submarine mountains of the four hundred fathom exterior ocean—all show but a repetition of the "detached hills rising from slightly elevated ground," the "peaked and serrated ridges," and isolated summits of the "large lateral spurs diverging from the chain, *especially* on its seaward side, which appear" like separate and independent mountain masses" rising out of the ocean low land, or, in the case of the submarine mountains, from the four hundred fathom floor of the Pacific plain. In this case I believe that the workings of the coral insect would be found, if examination were made, not to extend below the upper one hundred feet of these submarine mountains; ‖ perhaps our old friend, Captain Nares, with his scientific companions in H.M.S. "Challenger," may be able to settle the matter.

37. Four miles N. of the South Barnard Islands Nos. III., IV., V., and VI., islands of the group rear their scrub-clad hummocky backs—at night resembling a small herd of elephants disporting girth deep in the water. Of similar shape and appearance to the Southern Island, these islands, however, are formed of micaceous schist, with quartz veins and some galena, as described by Mr. McGillivray‡. The lead ore was found by me last year, but in too small quantities to pay. One of the quartz veins had a very auriferous appearance, although the actual "color" was not perceptible.

38. We anchored under No. III. Island at 5.30 p.m. on the 30th of September, in one quarter less three fathoms, broken coral and sandy bottom, one hundred yards from shore, the summit of the island bearing S.E.¼S., and Double Point N.W.¾W. Camp was formed on the S.W. sand spit, and the island was carefully examined by Mr. Hill, Mr. Johnstone, and myself. A small supply of fresh water was found trickling from the precipitous schist rocks on the south side. A good supply of Torres Straits pigeons were added to the larder, also several scrub hens (*Megapodius*). The latter is, however, a very tough dry bird, and not an acquisition to the table. Mr. Johnstone shot a number of fine specimens of the Victoria rifle bird, which were carefully skinned and preserved by Mr. Tompson.

39. From

* Voyage of H.M.S. "Rattlesnake," vol. I., p. 87.
† "A Sketch of the Physical Structure of Australia," pages 6–7.
‡ Voyage of H.M.S. "Rattlesnake," vol. I., p. 83.
‖ "Lyell's Principles of Geology," book III., p. 295.

8

39. From No. 3 Barnard Island, the contour of the next large coast basin, which it faces, was distinctly traced—bounded on the S. by the massive range spur running out towards Tam O'Shanter Point previously mentioned ; to the W., running back some thirty miles to the Main Coast Range N. of Cashmere ; and to the N.W. and N. bounded by the loftiest mountains in Queensland, the "Bellenden-Kerr Range," of 5,185 feet, and a more lofty and imposing mountain, 5,438 feet in height, S.S.W. of it, which I named Mount Bartle Frere, after Sir Bartle Frere of Indian and Zanzibar fame, now President of the Royal Geographical Society.

40. The whole of this great coast basin appeared to be densely wooded, and to contain the valleys of important streams.

41. The discovery, by Captain Moresby, of H.M.S. "Basilisk," of Mourilyan Harbor and the Moresby River, at once furnished this region with a seaport outlet, and the discovery by Mr. Sub-inspector Robert Johnstone, of the Native Mounted Police, early in 1873, of a fine river with rich soil and dense scrubs upon its banks, a few miles farther north, gave promise that here a new and valuable agricultural district was on the eve of discovery.

42. To thoroughly examine this district, it became necessary first to enter and explore Mourilyan Harbor, the River Moresby, and the land upon their shores—no other inlet from "Clump Point" to "Double Point" being found available.

MOURILYAN HARBOR AND MORESBY RIVER.

43. Camp was struck and all on board at 7·30 a.m. on the first of October, and we stood N.W. before a six-knot breeze for Mourilyan Harbor. The weather was beautifully clear, and the bold outlines of Mounts Bartle Frere, Bellenden Kerr and the inland Main Range, formed a fine background to the coast scenery.

44. From Double Point, which is rocky and openly timbered, a range of level-topped thickly-wooded hills rises from the sea, dividing it from the alluvial coast basins previously alluded to, as far as Cape Grafton, broken occasionally by the out-flow of their main drainage channels.

45. Passing under this range for four miles, one of these breaks opened out gradually to its full width of about 250 yards between two heads rising from a rocky shore of reddish micaceous schist, in two steep densely-wooded hills of about 300 feet elevation—the smooth waters of Mourilyan Harbor, with dark green hills beyond, appearing through this natural gateway.

46. It required the full strength of a fresh S.E. breeze to carry the cutters slowly in against an ebb tide, running out with the strength of current and deep-swirling eddies of a large salmon river.

47. Goodman's Rocks showed a jagged and ugly profile above the rushing tide on the starboard side. Just within them we discovered a dangerous outlying rock, named "Perry's Rock," after its discoverer. It lies about fifty yards from the south shore towards the fairway, which is here not above 120 yards broad, and through which we carried five fathoms at half-ebb.

48. Rounding Camp Point—the inner point of the south shore, the whole smooth expanse of this pretty little harbor spread away for about a mile to the two entrances to the Moresby River, visible at the south end, and up which several canoes full of blacks were seen making the best of their way to a place of safety.

49. On the E., N., and W., the harbor is picturesquely bounded by the dark-wooded Georgie, Hilda, and Ethel hills of Captain Moresby's survey. On the S.E., a low grassy hill, green as an emerald, I named "Esmeralda Hill ;" and a pretty wooded one between it and the sea, "Mount Julia." These hills are divided from Georgie Hill by a short valley running out from the shores of the harbor upon pretty grassy slopes and a smooth sandy beach between "Double Point" and "Hayter's Point," which I named "Seaforth Vale." In it, abundance of fresh water was discovered, and many beautiful building sites are to be found on its slopes both towards the harbor and the ocean, the distance across being only about three-quarters of a mile.

50. The first appearance of Mourilyan Harbor, both as to scenery and utility for commercial purposes, is undoubtedly prepossessing. Not only is it completely land locked, but we carried five fathoms in, deepening to twelve, ten, nine, eight, seven fathoms up to our anchorage, about forty feet from the shore at Camp Point, and the whaleboat got two and a-half fathoms a boat's length from the shore inside of us.

51. The broad opening of the Moresby River gave promise of a good water way to the S.W. back country of the great coast basin, and Walter's Creek to the western portion.

52. The camp was pitched on a most picturesque knoll at Camp Point, under the dark shade of wide-spreading fig-trees, on the site of a blacks' main camp, some of their bark and palm-leaf gunyahs still standing. Good water was found on both sides, trickling down fresh and cold out of George Hill.

53. A more convenient or picturesque site it would be difficult to find, and at night, in the moonlight, the view of the harbor and cutters at anchor with their lights up, as seen through the archway of dark fig-tree foliage, was at once beautiful and thoroughly tropical in its character.

54. Each night during our stay Mr. Hall, of the "Flying Fish," caught a plentiful supply of the largest mullet we had ever seen, besides black bream, &c.

55. In the dense scrubs, or rather jungles, to which descend the surrounding hills to the water's edge, we were for the first time introduced to *true tropical Queensland*, and to a development of vegetation thoroughly oriental in its character, and unlike any other in the Australian Colonies.

56. The hills around Mourilyan Harbor possess a richness of soil, a denseness of jungle, and a general gradient of slope which will render them very valuable for coffee plantations. The uninitiated in this industry are of opinion that any good soil, with even plains or open forest upon it, will grow coffee ; but the practical planter knows that it can only be carried on profitably in the rich vegetable loams (mixed with the detritus of volcanic tuffs, limestones, or schists, granites, &c.), only found in virgin forests such as those of the central mountain zones of Ceylon, Java, or Jamaica. I consider that the coffee lands of the N.E. coast of Queensland, which we have just explored, are quite equal to any of these, and I believe that climatic influences will tend to the production of a berry of very superior quality and value. The question of coffee growth within the influence of the sea breeze is simply one of climate, regulated by latitude, elevation, and ocean currents. In Ceylon, which is in 7° N. as well as in Jamaica, which

which is in 17° N., low class coffees only are grown near the coast; the zone of production of the high class plantation sorts extends from about 2,500 feet to the frost line at about 4,000 feet above the ocean, the climate of the latter being equalized with that of Ceylon by the influences of the Gulf Stream sweeping round its shores from the Caribbean Sea into the Gulf of Mexico. In the same latitude however (17° S.), on the N.E. coast of Queensland, in the vicinity of Cardwell, coffee grows luxuriantly and produces heavily on the sea level, as well as on the mountains at 1,100 feet, at which elevation I planted three dozen seedlings, experimentally, in November, 1872. There is a small flourishing plantation in the Brisbane Botanical Gardens, very near sea level, producing well shaped beans. It would be advisable to send samples of the produce of these several localities to England for classification and report by East India brokers for the information of future planters.

57. I ascended Esmeralda Hill, and from its open summit obtained a comprehensive view of Mourilyan Harbor and the whole of the great valley or basin embraced by its lateral mountain arms, and extending thirty miles back to the watershed range of the Mitchell and Herbert rivers.

58. On Thursday, October 2nd, I proceeded up the Moresby River with Mr. Johnstone and five troopers in the whaleboat, Mr. Hill accompanying us with Mr. Nind in his boat.

59. Sounding from Camp Point into the river, I found that the banks have shifted since Captain Moresby's survey. Where one fathom, and one and a-half, and one and three-quarter fathoms are entered on sheet XVI. of the Admiralty Chart, I only obtained three feet at low water "springs," the sand bank extending right across the channel.

60. Entering the river, the depth improved, corresponding with the chart soundings, and we followed it up for sixteen miles as therein laid down, from the survey by the officers of H.M.S.S. "Basilisk," until it became a mere mangrove creek too narrow to allow the oars to work.

61. From mouth to head the banks of the river were almost entirely a continuation of dense mangroves. At two places only, on the south bank, small tracts of open worthless tea-tree country occurred. On the north bank three belts of higher ground, clothed with dense vine and lawyer jungles, broke the monotonous uniformity of the mangroves.

62. We landed on these, and found the soil to be a rich red loam of great depth (vide soil sample No. 2), as shown by the section cutting of the bank. These belts evidently connected with large areas of similar character to the rear, and will not only themselves be valuable for agricultural purposes, but by this connection will give this river a commercial value to which otherwise it could lay no claim.

63. Near the head of boat navigation Mr. Nind discovered a very beautiful new tree orchid with a stem some seven feet long.

64. During our stay in Mourilyan Harbor Mr. Hill, protected by the native police, made a large collection of botanical treasures.

65. Mr. Johnstone obtained two specimens of the female of the Victoria rifle bird, and a black bird with yellow bill and feet, about the size of the mutton bird, which was unknown to us.

66. Hilda Hill, on the north side of the harbor, I found to have a rich reddish loam, the rocks beneath being chloritic mica slate; at the base of the hill, on the harbor, ferruginous slates occurred, with ferruginous chloritic mica slate. Ethel Hill was found to be formed of rotten mica slate, penetrated by quartz veins. Georgie Hill is of the same formation as Hilda Hill, on the opposite side of the harbor entrance. On its eastern sea face, near high-water mark, a vein of quartz with manganese and iron ore, occurred. A large quartz reef, running E. by W., was found crossing Esmeralda Hill, but had generally a barren appearance, although detached blocks looked more encouraging for gold prospecting.

67. I rigged a tide gauge at Camp Point, which showed a rise and fall of seven feet during our stay—the ebb and flood coursing in and out of the narrow entrance with great force, showing the necessity for sailing vessels to strictly adhere to the sailing directions in "Pugh's Almanack," viz. :—"Sailing vessels should not attempt to enter except with a fair and commanding breeze."

68. Once within the port, three men-of-war can swing in the ten and twelve-fathom basin, and there is natural wharfage along the north and east shores for the amount of shipping at present making use of the Port of Brisbane.

69. Scrub turkeys were numerous. The tracks of many cassowaries and of a wild or tiger-cat, similar to that which Mr. Johnstone, Mr. Armit, and the troopers of my party saw in the Rockingham Ranges in 1872, were frequent in the hill jungles. Crocodiles were seen in the harbor.

70. There is suitable ground on the lower slopes of Hilda Hill, to the water's edge on the north shore and round the western base of that hill, and also along the harbor at the base of Georgie Hill and through Seaforth Vale to the sea, for a township site—its warehouses and shops, &c., along the quay frontages; the private residences, as before stated, stretched seaward along Georgie Hill, Mount Julia, and Esmeralda Hill.

71. From the southern base of Mount Julia and Esmeralda Hill, open forest country extends along the coast to "Bay Hill" and "Double Hill," with a width inland from the beach of about two to three miles. Although apparently inferior country, yet its proximity to the probable township site will make it valuable as the only grazing country within reach, as well as a possible route from the south for the passage of stock for the support of the townspeople and planting community of the district.

72. In the annexed chart, I have marked such areas as it appeared to me to be advisable to recommend for reservation for town sites; also a portion of the above-mentioned grazing land as a pastoral commonage, there being none other in the neighborhood.

GLADY'S INLET AND THE RIVER "JOHNSTONE."

73. On Saturday, the 4th of October, camp was struck, all on board by 8 a.m., and instructions issued to Mr. Tompson, who was left in charge, and to the masters of the cutters, to follow me to the entrance of Mr. Johnstone's new river, six miles down the coast N.N.W., and to "lay-to" off the bar until signalled to stand in.

74. With Mr. Johnstone, Perry, and crew of Native Mounted Police I sailed down the coast in the whaleboat to sound the entrance to the valuable discovery of my companion.

75. The day was very fine, but hot. As the light land wind died away, about 9.30 a.m., a light S.E. breeze came up and bore us along under the wooded coast range which rose from wave-washed rocks

B   of of reddish, ferruginous mica-schist, to the height of 300 to 800 feet. This range extends from the north head of Mourilyan Harbor to the south side of Johnstone's River mouth, and received the name of Moresby's Range after the gallant commander of H.M.S.S. "Basilisk," as being connected with his discoveries and surveys on this portion of the coast.

76. In four miles we rounded a rocky grass-topped headland, whence the coast line receded into a broad shoal estuary—Moresby Range falling away on the south side and the hills recommencing on the northern shore, similarly clothed with dense woodlands, and rising to the superior elevations of 1,638 and 1,114 feet. This coast range, situated as described under head 41 of this Report, I named "Seymour's Range," after my old and respected friend, the Commissioner of Police.

77. Sand-banks, with a white break over them, appeared to extend right across, as shown in the Admiralty chart of Glady's River, and running down outside the break, along the two-fathom line, a river mouth opened out in the N.W. corner of the estuary, and a channel through the banks developed itself.

78. It being low water, we carried only three feet over the bar, deepening to four feet off a long rocky point on the north shore, three-quarters of a mile in which was named "Flying Fish Point."

79. At one and a-quarter miles in, or half-a-mile within Flying Fish Point, the water deepened to eight and nine feet, and as the second spit of the river mouth, named "Coquette Point," was approached, to two, three, and four fathoms close up to the point.

80. Up to this point we were under the belief that we were entering Glady's River, especially as the entrance of both is in latitude 17° 30′ S., and longitude 146° 0′ E. Here, however, all features of possible identity disappeared.

81. Instead of entering a narrow river, with an average depth of six or eight feet, with a "sluggish" stream, "but fresh to within a few hundred yards of the bar,"* we found a broad deep river with soundings from two to eight fathoms for fifteen miles, fresh water only commencing at eight miles from the entrance, and a tide, which, at both ebb and flow, has a rapid current, especially at the entrance, where it partakes more of the character of that of Mourilyan Harbor (vide head 47 of this Report).

82. I therefore considered that I was justified in naming the river after Mr. Johnstone, a gentleman who has become identified with enterprise and discovery on the N.E. coast, and who first brought to light the real character and value of this fine river, and its rich agricultural lands.

83. I have the honor to suggest as a means of recognising that gentleman's services, without, I sincerely trust, any possible injustice or discourtesy to the officers of H.M.S.S. "Basilisk," that the river having been entered, examined, and faithfully reported on last year, by Mr. Johnstone, be called by his name, and that its estuary, which was examined by Captain Moresby, be called "Glady's Inlet."

84. Two fathoms were obtained a boat's length off Coquette Point, deepening to five fathoms off Perry's Point, which forms the north head of the entrance. Some rocks inside Perry's Point contract the mouth to about 250 yards in breadth, with a deep and rapid current at both ebb and flood.

85. The dense jungles and sound rich soil come down to the water's edge, a little above Perry's Point, giving place to a narrow mangrove belt on the north or left bank for about a mile up the river.

86. Inside the entrance the river expanded to an imposing breadth, and three and four fathoms were obtained over most part of the first reach up to the Crocodile Rocks, which shew six feet out of water at low tide, but are covered at three-quarter flood, and are situated on the north side at the head of the reach at the first bend.

87. Coquette Point presented a suitable site for camp; we therefore sounded straight out over the bar to the cutters, which had arrived and awaited us, and took them in with a fair wind, carrying six and seven feet over the banks at half-flood. A slight break remaining on the north and south banks on either side showed the channel to be about 300 yards wide.

88. We anchored close under Coquette Point, in four fathoms, sand and mud bottom, and formed camp on the open grassy space above the sand spit.

89. Numbers of blacks were seen on the beaches of the estuary, north and south of the river mouth, and three very neat bark canoes were found drawn up on Perry's Point.

90. The smaller raft of the ill-fated brig "Maria," of the New Guinea Expedition, was washed ashore in this estuary, and nine unarmed helpless starving Englishmen were murdered in cold blood by these bloodthirsty savages, on the adjacent beaches. One poor fellow had been found nearly cut in pieces, and had been buried close to our camp by Mr. Johnstone and the volunteers of the s.s. "Governor Blackall."

91. A tide gauge was rigged on Coquette Point, and spring tides being on, we registered nine feet and eight feet six inches, rise and fall, on the night of the full moon and one preceding it.

92. An abundant supply of excellent fresh running water was procured by the "dingy" up a narrow creek on the north side just inside "Perry's Point." Abundance of water is also procurable on the south side, three-quarters of a mile from Coquette Point, behind the beach.

93. The south bank of the river slopes very gradually for about a mile to the north end of Moresby Range, having a natural wharfage with deep water along its western river frontage for two miles from the bend opposite Crocodile Rocks upwards.

94. The north shore slopes upwards more rapidly from Perry's Point to Mount Maria and Mount Annie (of 1,114 feet)—conspicuous peaks of Seymour's Range, which, with Mount Arthur, are named after members of Mr. Johnstone's family.

95. Natural wharfage, with two fathoms close up, will afford berths for four or five one-hundred ton vessels inside Perry's Point. The above land on both banks is well situated for townships, and good building sites for private residences, facing the sea breeze, are plentiful on the slopes of Moresby's and Seymour's ranges; I have therefore considered it advisable to recommend for reservation for public purposes the lands marked on the annexed chart embracing these localities.

96. Our indefatigable fisherman, Hall, provided us daily with a good supply of fine large silver bream and other fish, and reported that quantities of very large Mullet and Barramunda leaped over his net or went through it like a cobweb.

97. From

---

* "Sailing Directions," Pugh's Almanack for 1874, page 288.

11

97. From our camp the towering mass of "Mount Bartle Frere" was an imposing feature to the westward, distant direct about fifteen miles.

98. On Sunday, the 5th of October, I despatched Messrs. Johnstone and Hill, accompanied by Mr. Nind, to select a good central camping place and anchorage for the exploration of the main and south branches of the river, and at 11 a.m., as usual, service was read on the deck of the "Flying Fish."

99. In the afternoon Mr. Johnstone returned, having found a suitable camping place at the junction of the main and south branches. Mr. Nind remained there, and cleared a sufficient area for the camp. Messrs. Johnstone and Hill spoke in high terms of the size and depth of the river, and the richness of soil and jungles on its banks.

100. At daybreak on Monday, the 6th of October, the tents were struck, all were on board by 5·45 a.m., and the cutters, propelled by their sweeps and a strong flood tide, followed the whaleboat, which sounded ahead as usual, the soundings and bearings being duly recorded.

101. About a quarter of a mile from Coquette Point, at Crocodile Rocks, the river turns suddenly to the south, and half-a-mile farther to the S.E., carrying two, three, four, five, and six fathoms, with a channel as broad as the Brisbane from Galloway's Hill to Newstead.

102. At about two and a-half miles from Coquette Point it again sweeps round W.S.W. into a fine reach of about three miles in length, and as broad as the Brisbane between Newstead and Lytton. At the head of the reach Mr. Nind's tents were conspicuous in mid channel at the fork or junction of the north and south branches.

103. Near the bend at the east end of the reach a deep creek entered on the south or right bank from the direction of Mourilyan Harbor, which from this point cannot be farther, direct, than five miles.

104. The average soundings of the three-mile reach were about eight feet, except about half-a-mile below the "Junction," where a sand bank with five feet and four feet extended from the N. bank up to "Banana Island," of about 300 yards long, of rich soil covered with wild palms, bananas, and jungle. This island is again divided from the S. bank by a channel fifty yards wide, with better soundings by two feet throughout.

105. Both banks of the river were generally well elevated above the water, showed a soil of unsurpassable richness, and were clothed with a dense and luxuriant jungle ; palms and wild bananas forming frequent masses of brightest green.

106. We anchored at "Nind's Junction Camp," at 7·10 a.m., within the south branch in two fathoms, a boat's length off the shore, sand and mud bottom.

107. Camp was formed on shore, and Mr. Nind's kindness in clearing the site was highly appreciated ; in fact, since we had the pleasure of that gentleman's company on his venturesome expedition down this coast, in a small boat with four men, nothing could exceed his courtesy and unostentatious offers of assistance on all occasions.

108. Mr. Nind reported that a large number of blacks had been cooeeing round his camp during the night.

109. At 8 a.m. I started in the whaleboat with Mr. Johnstone and crew of Native Mounted Police, and Perry taking the soundings, and accompanied by Mr. Nind in his boat with Mr. Hill with some more Native Mounted Troopers. Ascended the south branch of the river in a general S.W. direction, though somewhat winding course, for about ten miles.

110. For the first six miles its breadth equalled that of the Brisbane between Oxley Creek and Woogaroo, its character as a navigable stream resembling the Herbert, but with better soundings; at high water a vessel drawing six feet of water can ascend without difficulty for eight miles from the junction.

111. About half-a-mile above Nind's Camp, the water was fresh at low tide, at eight miles up it was quite fresh at high-water springs.

112. Close to Nind's Camp quartz rock with mica, micaceous slate, and talcous schist, cropped out on the river bank. At eight miles up rocks of a ferruginous conglomerate contracted the channel; above this its width was similar to that of the Bremer at its junction with the Brisbane.

113. About a mile and a-half farther up, rapids over shingle and stones occurred, over which at low water the boats proceeded with difficulty; above them, however, the stream again assumed a deeper character, and passed through a sort of cutting of volcanic tufa (vide rock specimen B No. 9) for some distance.

114. Returning down stream in the evening at low water, sand banks were found to extend across at two islands covered with beautiful jungle about one and two miles respectively from the junction, and over these banks we had only two feet of water.

115. The banks of this branch average twelve to twenty feet above the water and show sections of rich chocolate-colored loam of great depth, on substrata of volcanic tuffs, yellow ochre, ferruginous conglomerate, ferruginous sandstone, and micaceous slates. Mr. Hill penetrated some distance from the river banks and obtained specimens of the soils (vide soil specimens "Collection No. 2, bags Nos. 2 to 10, now in the Brisbane Government Museum).*

116. The banks of the river and as far back as it was possible to penetrate with the time at our disposal, and the amount of work before us at so late a period of the season, during which alone such coasting work is safe on this coast, showed a continuous succession of the loftiest and densest tropical growth in Australia, one mass of large forest trees and thick undergrowth of palms, "lawyers," and groves of wild bananas, the former festooned in gorgeous drapery of canes, creeping bamboos, and richly flowering creepers in full bloom. Only in the alluvial valleys of India, the Malayan Archipelago, and South America, is such luxuriance and beauty of growth to be found.

117. We were fortunate in discovering red cedar of good quality—one tree near the river bank, from which Mr. Hill took a sample block, measured twenty-three feet nine inches in girth at three feet from the ground.

118. Good fire-brick clay and slates were also found, and will be invaluable to future settlers on the river.

119. The sand and gravel of the river bed are disintegrated granite, with abundance of small waterworn quartz pebbles and mica ; but, on trial with the tin dish, did not give "the color."

120. On

---

* Duplicate specimens are about to be sent home by Mr. Staiger, per "Indus," to Mr. Daintree.

120. On Tuesday, the 7th of October, at 8 a.m., we again started up the south branch with the determination of either reaching open country beyond the jungles or of ascending a range of hills seen from our highest point of ascent of the Moresby River, and from our highest point reached yesterday.

121. The police whaleboat, although a fine sea-boat, being too heavy and of too deep draught of water for shallow river work, Mr. Nind kindly took me in his boat, which was lighter and drew less water, with a crew of Native Mounted Police—Mr. Johnstone and Mr. Hill accompanying us in the dingy, with a crew of Native Mounted Police also.

122. Three miles up the river, on the east bank, the smoke of a black's camp curled up above the jungle. Mr. Johnstone landed to examine it, and found it just vacated. He found in the camp a very superior and nearly new American axe, which must have been taken from the murdered men of the "Maria's" raft. Fine blue slates were found in this camp.

123. Ascending the river with the flood tide, we carried three feet of water over the shingly rapids which we had crossed with difficulty the day before.

124. We succeeded in accomplishing three miles of ascent beyond our limit of yesterday, carrying the same character of stream and high banks of rich soil clad with exactly the same dense jungles.

125. At the head of boat navigation (twelve miles above Nind's Junction Camp) the river contracted to about fifty yards, and rapids like a Scotch trout stream occurred over a shingly bottom, over which it was impossible to track the boats without injuring them for future service; and, seeing the low range referred to (under head 114 of this report) apparently about two miles south, we landed. Mr. Nind, one of his men, and three Native Mounted Police remained with the boats, and I proceeded with Mr. Johnstone and Mr. Hill, and, accompanied by four Native Mounted Police troopers, cut our way with machetes (sugar-knives) and tomahawks through the dense jungle, and ascended the north point of the range, which rose steep to a nearly bare grassy crown of about 350 feet above the sea.

126. From the summit a magnificent—and for the purposes of the Expedition—a most useful and comprehensive view was obtained.

127. A round of compass bearings was at once secured, including the Barnard Islands, Double Point, Mourilyan Harbor—clearly seen to the eastward (the southerly course of the South Johnstone having brought us to a point due west of Esmeralda Hill), and the hills at the mouth of the Johnstone River. Bellenden Kerr Mountains were shrouded in dense clouds of smokes of blacks' fires, but the lofty peak of Mount Bartle Frere cut the clear blue sky to the N.W. far above them. Thence, W. and S., ranges beyond ranges bounded the great coast basin, the whole of the wide-spread floor of which presented one vast unbroken expanse of dense tropical jungles; no differing shades or outlines permitting of any other opinion than that the vegetation and soil over the whole of this magnificent area were of exactly the same character and quality as that immediately around us.

128. At a rough computation, not less than half-a-million of acres of a soil unsurpassed by any in the world—all fitted for tropical agriculture, and fully 300,000 acres of which are suitable for sugar—spread far around us, penetrated in three different directions by navigable rivers, with a fine harbor and river estuary visible on its sea-board. We had suddenly come face to face with a true tropical Australia—with a vast and hitherto hidden region, the qualifications of which for every description of tropical cultivation at one stroke place our noble colony not only far beyond all Australian competition as an agricultural country, but—the vexed labor question settled—on a par with older tropical countries, the names and products of which are household words.

129. I use Mr. Hill's words when I say that "the soil cannot be surpassed;" that it is "the most valuable discovery in Australia." Such expressions from so practical a horticulturist speak for themselves.

130. The general appearance of the country was that of a great level basin, rising gently from the river channels in low gradations or steps, broad, level, or very gently sloping back to the mountains, which were clothed with jungles as dense as those which covered the whole country as far as the eye could reach.

131. We were loath to descend into the dark dank jungles again from the bright hill-top daylight, and from the grand and interesting view of a discovery with which our hearts bounded with gratification to think that our names had become suddenly associated. It was one of those moments which only the explorer knows, and which repay him for many hardships and weary days of toil.

132. As an evidence of the density of the jungles, I may mention that it took three hours' hard cutting to traverse that which intervened between the boats and the hill; and we retraced the distance—about two miles—in an hour.

133. From our hill of observation, the massive lateral spur of the Main Range running out towards Tam O'Shanter Point, as described under heading 14 of this Report, formed an imposing boundary to the southward, and is equally conspicuous from Cardwell, and in sailing along the coast.

134. Mr. Walter Hill, by exploration of the rich alluvial lands north and south of this range, has honorably connected his name with it. I therefore took the opportunity, on the top of our Observation Hill, of naming it "Walter Hill's Ranges," a name which I trust the Government will confirm; a compliment which, on the spot, Mr. Hill warmly appreciated.

135. Our Observation Hill is the northern mountain headland of a spur of Walter Hill's Ranges, standing boldly out into the sea of low country jungles. It forms the watershed ridge between the South Johnstone and Mourilyan Harbor, and being a connecting link with the surveys of Captain Moresby, R.N., on the latter, I have given it the distinctive name of " Basilisk Range."

136. An east and west quartz reef outcrop ran completely over Observation Hill, and appeared to run due east towards that found on Esmeralda Hill or Mourilyan Harbor. No color of gold was obtained in that, or from the wash dirt from under the river bank at the boats, which was tried in the tin dish; but, from the quantities of black sand and small quartz pebbles, mica, slates, and quartz leaders of rather promising appearance, I have great hopes that gold may be found on the eastern slopes of the Main Range, at the heads of these rivers.

137. When descending the hill, Mr. Johnstone shot a fine scrub turkey *(Thlagolla)*.

138. Mr. Hill found, and brought away, specimens of a new, very stately, and handsome banana, the stem of which was thirty feet in height, three feet six inches in girth, and of a dark polished mahogany color ; the fruit, however, though ripe, was hard, tough, and full of seeds.

139. Although

13

139. Although quite dark, we pulled all the way down the river to camp, at a good pace, without touching on the flats, and arrived at nine p.m.

140. On Tuesday, the 7th of October, I remained on board to arrange and pack mineral and soil specimens, write up the log, journal, and enter soundings, cross bearings, and meteorological observations—duties which devolved entirely upon me, and which, with the taking of the soundings and bearings in the boats, the observations of the instruments, and general direction of the Expedition, completely occupied my time.

141. I despatched Mr. Tompson, with Mr. Johnstone and Mr. Hill, to explore the country for some distance back from the river. They found the soil and vegetation to be all alike; having penetrated a mile from the river, and ascended a creek (Bamboo Creek, on which Mr. Hill had first found the wild bamboo), and which joins the South Johnstone, half-a-mile above Nind's Camp, on the left bank.

142. To sum up the characteristics of the south branch, besides the existence of cedar, twenty-three feet in girth; wild bananas, thirty feet high, and three feet six inches in girth; and wild bamboo, over 200 feet in length; the wild ginger, a plant which, further south, we can tread under foot, and here measured nineteen feet in height, are sufficient evidence of the capabilities of the soil, and permit of sanguine expectations for the future of this fine district.

143. Turning our boats' heads from their berth in the south branch out into the main river, on the morning of Thursday, the 9th of October, we were struck with the breadth and bold sweep of the reaches, which one after another unfolded themselves, mile upon mile, as we ascended it.

144. In some of the bends no soundings were obtained with seven and nine fathoms of line. In the straight reaches nothing under two fathoms was obtained for about nine miles, the breadth throughout the whole of this distance equalling that of the Brisbane reach, between Galloway's Hill and Newstead.

145. The character of the banks was found to be similar to those on the south branch, but in places far exceeding them in the magnificent luxuriance of the vegetation.

146. On the north bank, the land was generally high, above all possibility of flooding. The steep banks of dark-brown and reddish loam of twenty to forty feet in height, clothed with dense masses of lofty forest, heavily festooned with flowering creepers of convolvuli, climbing bamboo, and lawyer palms, descend to the water's edge, in steep slopes of luxuriant entanglement and variety of undergrowth; palms, bananas, ferns, lilies, arums, and large-leaved tara, struggling for prominence of position,—a dazzling commingling of shades, colors, and intricate minutiæ of outline that would puzzle even a Millais to paint or a "Laureate" to describe; the deliciously scented acums, all in full bloom, and hanging moon-flowers greeting us, as we passed, with whole greenhouses of rich perfume.

147. At two miles, we passed an island covered with the same dense, lofty vegetation.

148. For the first four miles, the jungles of the north or left bank rose with gently-ascending slopes and low terraces to the hills of the back of Seymour's Coast Range—Mounts Arthur and Annie being conspicuous objects—and through their valleys, down to the ocean beyond, Bellenden-Kerr Mountains being visible to the N.N.W., massive and blue.

149. At five and a-half miles up, the pyramidal-shaped hill which forms the leading land-mark for entering the river came in sight up a westerly reach, and immediately afterwards, the peculiar horn-like southern bluff of Mount Bartle Frere afforded us a prominent object for a compass bearing, ere the clouds of a heavy S.E. rain squall, just breaking upon us, enveloped all in gloom.

150. At seven miles from the junction, at the bend of a N.W. reach, the gunyahs of a large blacks' camp came in sight on a high, bare, level bank.

151. Landing and ascending to the camp, which was deserted, a curious scene presented itself. The flat-topped ridge, elevated about fifteen feet above the river, ran out to a point, bounded on either side by the river and a deep tributary creek from the N.W. The whole area of the top was swept perfectly clean over a space fifty yards by sixty-four yards, and beaten hard by the hundreds of stamping feet of many successive mobs of blacks who have here held their "bora" meetings and corrobories for many a day. To suddenly come in sight, up the reach, of such a gathering in the dark night—the ruddy glow of the camp fires lighting up the swarthy, dancing savages in their war paint, accompanied by the yells and gutterals of their war corrobories—would be a scene indescribably wild and picturesque.

152. A row of bark and palm-leaf huts extended across the land side of this aboriginal parade ground, shaded by some very fine fig-trees, sand, box, and Moreton Bay chesnuts. A large, well-painted, wooden shield was found. These blacks have certainly, as they frequently do, selected a most picturesque and commanding site for their head-quarters' camp; this one being placed at a sharp bend of the river, whence a beautiful view is obtained up and down two reaches—the first for a mile and a-half, the second for a mile.

153. This bora ground afforded evidence of the large numbers of blacks in this locality, further borne out by the numerous catamarans or rafts, made of three logs of light timber or banana stems lashed together with strips of cane, and capable of carrying five or six people, which we saw moored along the river banks. We saw twenty between our junction camp and the bora ground, and remarked that they were all moored on the side next the camp—evidence of a curiosity on the part of their owners which might prove inconvenient to us in our daily explorations.

154. About nine miles from the junction and two miles above the bora camp, another pretty island occupied the centre of the stream, which here narrowed to the width of the Brisbane at the Bremer Junction. I named it Ferny Island, its banks sloping down to the water, a mass of beautiful ferns.

155. Here a bar of rock crosses the river, reducing the soundings at one place to five feet; but immediately above it again we had four and five fathoms.

156. The rain coming down in torrents, we turned at Ferny Bank Point, just above the island, and equally covered with ferns, and returned to camp.

157. Although there was a rise and fall of tide of four to six feet up the river, there was but little current either way from two miles above the junction—the flood tides apparently simply banking up the fresh water, and forcing it back upon its course.

158. The highest flood marks observed were about fifteen feet, and the banks of the river generally much exceed that elevation.

159. Having determined to move the Expedition up to Bora Camp, thence to complete the exploration of the upper course of the river, the camp equipage and party were all on board at 9 a.m. on Friday, the 10th October, and the cutters stood up the river with a fresh S.E. breeze and fine weather.

160. All

160. All the catamarans were still on the camp side of the river, and more had joined them.

161. Rounding the bend into Bora Camp reach, a numerous black mob occupied the bora ground. They fled as we approached, and left several large catamarans, on which they had come down the river, moored alongside the bank. From the combined circumstances, we were of opinion that they were collecting to attack us; and the general impression was that the sooner they did so and discovered the full extent of their mistake, the better for us and for future settlers on these rivers.

162. The cutters dropped their anchors in seven fathoms, with sandy and muddy bottom, about twenty feet from the shore. The tents were pitched on the bora ground, and Mr. Johnstone and detachment of Native Police proceeded to patrol the neighboring dense jungles.

163. There were found in and around the camp, dropped by the blacks, in the haste of departure, shields, wooden swords, similar to those used in Rockingham Bay; dilly bags containing war paints, nets, fishing lines, and hooks; a dilly basket full of human bones and skulls, and several packages of stuff tied up in banana leaves, and having the appearance of pounded potatoes, probably made by the gins from the Tara which covers hundreds of acres in strips along the river banks, the leaf being exactly similar to some from the South Seas in the Brisbane Botanical Gardens. These Tara beds were here and there grubbed up over considerable patches by the blacks.

164. Mr. Johnstone and his troopers found blacks up trees across the creek watching the camp, and at midnight he and Mr. Nind, having the middle watch, heard the stealthy tread of feet cracking sticks in their advance through the dense darkness of the jungle towards the camp. The camp was quietly roused, and a volley from the sniders rattled through the underwood, succeeded by a more rapid and unmistakeable cracking of sticks by the flying feet of many retreating savages. In the morning, the tracks of a considerable "mob" were found close to the camp, and the same tracks in rapid retreat to the back creek, which they had swum, leaving swords and shields behind in their precipitate flight.

165. On the morning of the 11th of October, when preparing to start in the boats, to examine the upper course of the river, another mob of blacks came upon the river banks in a threatening manner, which was extremely inconvenient, as our departure would necessarily leave the camp more easily assailable. Their leader, a very tall and burly savage, swam half-way across the river, and was taken down by a crocodile.

166. I then proceeded up the river, in the whaleboat, accompanied by Mr. Nind, **Perry (sounding)**, and crew of Native Mounted Police. Mr. Hill was suffering severely from a bad **attack of fever and** unable to accompany me, and Mr. Johnstone remained in camp, **by my desire, to patrol and endeavor** to obtain specimens of rare birds.

167. Passing "Fency Bank Point," in three fathoms of water, the banks were high and of the same rich loam and splendid vegetation; when suddenly, to our surprise and disappointment, the river shoaled to three feet, shingly bottom and rapid stream, and in a mile a steep rapid barred our progress, and fixed the limit of boat navigation at low water; although with spring tides probably two miles farther may be accomplished: at present, however, I considered that the boat would be injured for future work by attempting it.

168. The river thence appears to come from the S.W., its general course from the mouth, a distance of about fifteen miles, having been about W.N.W.

169. All hopes of reaching Mount Bartle Frere, and ascending the highest mountain in Queensland, were as suddenly dissipated, its lowest spurs being evidently some eight miles distant, through dense jungles, which also ascend and clothe it to its summit.

170. From the top of the first rapids the river makes a complete horse-shoe bend, and across the narrowest part of the arc is the open grassy filled-up channel of an old bed, forming an escape for flood waters, and showing wreck marks on the trees fifteen feet high.

171. Entering a small inlet—the only part of this original water channel remaining—we landed and tried the wash-dirt from two feet below the surface, and in four dishes panned, obtained very decided color of gold, which, although small, was water worn, shotty, and of rich color. (Vide sample bag C., No. 6.)

172. Probably better results would be obtained on the bottom, but the wash-dirt was evidently deep, perhaps eight or ten feet, and we had no means of keeping the water out sufficiently to sink a hole and bottom. Most probably the matrix of the gold is in the watershed ranges of the Johnstone, Herbert, and Mitchell rivers; along which prospectors will, doubtless, soon discover payable deposits.

173. We returned to camp, where, the following day, Sunday, was kept as a day of rest and service, read under the pleasant shade of the large trees on this old scene of cannibalism and savage rites.

174. On Monday, the 13th of October, having thus completed the exploration of both branches of this fine river, fixed its navigable capabilities, and established the extent and richness of soil of the first great coast basin, to my satisfaction, the expeditionary party were all on board at daylight, and the cutters returned to and anchored in their old berths under Coquette Point. The day being very fine and clear afforded an excellent opportunity to correct the cross bearings for fixing the bends of the river and directions of its course by the prismatic compass.

175. On Tuesday, the 14th of October, camp was struck and all on board, and the cutters under weigh and standing out of the river with a fresh land breeze from W.S.W. Mr. Johnstone accompanied me, ahead of them in the whaleboat. Soundings were taken carrying seven feet right out over the bar at quarter ebb of a small neap tide of only six feet total rise.

176. The bar and channel, up to Coquette Point, are sandy bottom, and so even that a vessel drawing within only a few inches of the exact depth of water, would **meet no obstruction** if adhering to the course recommended, viz., W. by S. to Coquette Point.

177. It was high water at Coquette Point at the full **moon at 9·30** p.m., rise nine feet. Neap tides rise five feet to six feet average.

178. To admit vessels drawing over six feet **to the** deep water and fine reaches within Coquette Point, a channel would require to be dredged from the **outside** of the bar to within quarter of a mile of Coquette Point, a distance of one and a-quarter **miles**; and if the cutting were carried straight out I believe that the scour of the strong tides would keep it clear for some time; although undoubtedly the exposure of the entrance to the S.E. trades must always, sooner or later, bank up the mouth as before.

179. To allow vessels of deep draught to ascend to the deep water reaches above "Nind's Junction Camp," a similar cutting of half-a-mile in length would be required through the four feet sand bank at Banana Island.
180. Nind's

15

180. Ninel's Creek, however, having been proved navigable for small crafts for seven miles of a rather tortuous course, and to be only divided by a distance of some two miles from Captain Moresby's, Walter's Creek, navigable for similar vessels into Mourilyan Harbor; the advisability may arise in the future of connecting them by a canal, so as to bring the whole river traffic by water alongside ocean-going shipping in that port.

181. A railway or wooden tramway for light locomotives may, however, answer the purpose, connecting suitable water carriage near the junction of Ninel's Creek and the Johnstone, with the wharves on the north side of Mourilyan Harbor. In view of either of these means of communication I have marked the area of land necessary to be reserved for such purposes, in the accompanying chart.

182. From my observations of the formation of the basin of the Moresby and North and South Johnstone rivers, thus provided with extensive water carriage and a fine seaport, it became evident that the unusual richness of the soil was attributable to ages of deposit of decayed vegetable matter of primeval forests, upon, and mixing with decomposed strata of chloritic mica slates, talcous schists, ferruginous conglomerates, and volcanic tuffs and diorite, combined with a favorable humidity of the atmospheric currents, probably influenced by the position, loftiness, and massiveness of the coast ranges, which has produced a richness of vegetation unknown in other parts of Australia; and that, wherever, along the coast northwards, repetitions of these geological and atmospheric coincidences should occur, there the same rich soils and dense jungles will be found.

TRINITY HARBOR AND COAST FROM GLADY'S INLET TO MONKHOUSE POINT.

183. The breeze was fresh from the S.W. at 7 a.m., when we stood away for No. 1 of the Frankland Group, visible eighteen miles N.W.

184. A prominent headland two miles N. of Flying Fish Point, which will be a frequent future point of observation in making Glady's Inlet and the Johnstone River, I named "Heath Point," after Captain G. P. Heath, R.N., Portmaster of the colony.

185. Seymour's Range, of which Mounts Maria, Annie, and Arthur are the principal eminences, extends from the N. bank of the Johnstone to a little beyond Cooper Point, a bold headland seven miles N. of Glady's Inlet; woodlands and open glades alternating to its summit.

186. Along the seaside, Seymour's Range, alternately receding and again advancing its spurs towards the beach, encloses a succession of basins of rich jungle lands, connected with those on the Johnstone on the opposite side, and rendered more valuable from their proximity to open grassy ridges with good pasturage and fine open building sites facing the sea breeze.

187. When off Cooper Point we were becalmed for some hours, but a fresh N.E. breeze coming up with the young flood tide, we made a good anchorage under the W. side of No. 1 Frankland Island, at 3 p.m., coral and sandy bottom; the S. end of the island bearing N. 139° E., N. end of island bearing N. 34° N.E.

188. Camp was formed on the north end of the island, on the usual sand spit.

189. When standing in towards the island, and also from our anchorage, the broad mouth, evidently of an important river, was seen breaking the coast line under the centre of the Bellenden Kerr Range, which reared its long massive blue front to a rampart of crenulated peaks over 5,000 feet of abrupt ascent straight up from the sea.

190. Seymour's Range fell away three and a-half miles N.W. of Cooper Point, into a low valley connecting the seaward jungles with the Johnstone. Thence another range rising in one peak to an elevation of 2,195 feet, which I named "Graham's Range," after the late Honorable the Secretary for Public Lands, continued the extension of the Coast Range to the entrance of the river under Bellenden Kerr.

191. On the north bank of this river the Coast Range again rose to a considerable elevation, and was named "Malbon Thompson's Range." At its north extremity the geological formation changed to granite, and rose to the two lofty "Bell's Peaks," named after the Honorable J. P. Bell, of 3,357 feet and 3,032 feet respectively; the Coast Range being continued northwards by Grey's Peaks, of the Admiralty charts, Murray Prior's Peaks terminating in False Cape, in Trinity Bay, and N.E. of these hills, which are 2,710 feet in height; Grant Hill, Cape Grafton, and Fitzroy Island terminating the land line to the north.

192. Graham's and Malbon Thompson's Ranges appeared to be clothed with the same dense dark green jungles as those left behind us on Seymour's Range; the valleys between these ranges and the base of the Bellenden Kerr Range, which were apparently drained by the new river, appearing to be exactly the same character of country as that of the Johnstone River.

193. No. 1 Frankland Island is about a mile in diameter, lofty and jungle clad; at the south end, level, sandy, and scrubby to the N.W. It is the southern extremity of a line of steep rocky islets, connected by coral reefs, some of which on its N.E. side are extremely picturesque. The N.W. extremity of the group being a longer low island with a conspicuous rocky knoll at either extremity, the No. 2 Frankland of the charts.

194. At the S.E. end of No. 1, under which we were anchored, about two dozen fine cocoanuts, the only grove of these useful and graceful trees along the whole coast, nestled under the steepest part of the wooded hill; they are in full bearing and vigorous growth, and give quite an oriental character to the island.

195. Rounding the little headland, with its wave-washed diorite rocks and overhanging palms, reminded me of many a lovely shore view beneath the long canopy of cocoanut tops that shade some seventy miles of the coast road from Point de Galle to Colombo.

196. We sent the Native Police Troopers up the trees, and obtained a supply of ripe and drinking cocoanuts, the latter containing about a pint of water, which resembles delicately fruit-flavored eau sucré, and is a delicious and cool drink in the early morning.

197. The island at this season swarms with the white Torres Straits pigeons, which come off in the evening from the valley jungles of the new Bellenden Kerr River in hundreds of flocks. They feed in the daytime on the main land on jungle fruits, and roost at night on the outlying islands, and I have observed that the richness or barrenness of the coast lands may be pretty nearly estimated from the number of these pigeons then making their daily flights to and fro.

198. About forty pigeons and eight scrub hens (Megapodius) were brought on board in the evening, furnishing a pleasant change of fare.

199. Shortly after sundown a school of about twenty turtle of large size passed in a long line between

the

648

16

the cutters towards the shore, ploughing through the sea with considerable power and velocity, their great square heads throwing the water aside as from the rams of a miniature fleet of ironclads. Unfortunately the firing on shore frightened them out to sea, and none were found during the night on the island beaches.

200. On this little island camp no nightwatch was necessary on shore, but considering it advisable to make Fitzroy Island early next morning, fill up the watercasks there, and stand round into the bay W. of Cape Grafton for the night, the camp was astir at 3 a.m., all were on board and the cutters under weigh with a moderate E.S.E. breeze at 4 a.m.

201. Passing down the west side of the rocky islets terminating in No. 2 Frankland, and to the eastward of the lofty wooded high island of the group, the dawn broke through towering masses of clouds, and the rising sun lit up all the east with gorgeous masses of red and gold. Dark clouds brooded over the land, which was six miles off, and Bellenden Kerr was enveloped in a vast curtain of inky blackness down to his base, bringing out in stronger contrast the long line of white mist hanging low in the valleys between that mountain and Graham's and Malbon Thompson's ranges in front of him.

202. The short reference to this river in the Coast Sailing Directory, and its appearance on the Admiralty chart, were certainly not calculated to raise sanguine expectations; but the dark color and massiveness of the woodlands, the quantities of pigeons winging their flight towards the river mouth in the grey light of the morning, and the heavy white mists lying low in the valleys, raised strong hopes within me of as successful an issue to our exploration of this region on our return voyage, as had attended our exertions hitherto to the southward.

203. When abreast of Grey and Murray Prior's Peaks, the change from the schistose to granitic formation was very marked; now, the dense jungles and more rounded mountain outlines are succeeded by steep and sterile peaks, and mountain sides composed of masses of great slabs and outcrops of grey rock, with here and there scattered stunted timber.

204. With a fresh breeze, E. by N., we rounded the steep granite cliffs and more wooded slopes of Fitzroy Island, and anchored at 9 a.m. in a pretty, well-sheltered bay, with semicircular white sandy beach close under its N.W. side.

205. A watering party was landed in the whaleboat and dingy to fill up the watercasks from a clear running stream coming down a picturesque wooded glen, and percolating below through the high beach of broken coral, shells, and granite detritus, into the bay opposite the anchorage.

206. Here there is a recurrence of the old raised beaches and pumice pebbles rising in successive steps from the sea level, and affording the same evidences as previously stated, of either periodical and sudden upheavals of the land, or as sudden subsidences of the ocean. Regarding these coast phenomena—as alluded to under heads 33, 34, 35, and 36 of this narrative—from Mr. Mallet's point of view, viz., that of the internal cooling of the earth, and consequent contraction and subsidence of its crust, local evidences of which are evident at this day; it appears to me to be simpler to attribute them to such agencies rather than to the vagaries of upheaving forces, so gigantic as to be able to raise whole continents, and which, if existent within the earth, would inevitably have long since burst it into atoms, and hurled us to destruction.

207. The excellent anchorage and watering place appear to have been used some years since as a bêche-de-mer fishing station, and to be now a place of frequent call by vessels of that trade and passing ships.

208. It is melancholy to see the ruthless manner in which people from those vessels have destroyed magnificent calophyllum and fig trees, which originally formed a picturesque background to the beach, and grateful shade to landing parties. There is abundance of excellent firewood to be obtained close by. There are many other places along the coast where these despoilers have not yet commenced their ruthless destruction, but which will not long be safe if unprotected by legislative enactment; until this is done, even the beautiful cocoanut grove of the South Frankland Island is in peril.

209. At 11 a.m., having taken full supplies of wood and water on board, we got underweigh for the anchorage in the bay between Cape Grafton and False Cape.

210. At noon, our course was N.W. by W., strong breeze E. by N. with jumbling sea; Cape Grafton distant one mile on the port quarter.

211. At 1 p.m., we brought up under the west side of a small rocky island, with some bloodwood and ash trees on it, in the centre of the bay, and dropped anchors in two fathoms, sand and mud bottom; the N. point of the island bearing N. 70° E.; N. end of Green Island, N. 25° E.; False Cape, N. 277° W. The breeze was fresh from the eastward, and had evidently been blowing strong and continuously from that quarter out at sea, a heavy swell setting into the bay through Trinity Opening in the Great Barrier reefs, fifteen miles to the north.

212. Camp was, as usual, formed on the island. Many blacks were seen round the shores of the bay, from which steep scrubby hills rise on all sides, except to the south, where a dead level runs through to the sea on the opposite side, a distance of three and a-half miles. Blacks' camp fires burnt brightly during the night in glens of the mountain sides. The cutters rolled heavily all night.

213. On the morning of Thursday, the 16th October, I despatched Mr. Tompson in the whaleboat, with Messrs. Johnstone and Hill and crew of Native Police, to examine the low land at the south end of the bay. They returned at 9 a.m., and reported no navigable creek nor any good land to be seen.

214. At 10 a.m. I started in the whaleboat with crew of Native Mounted Police to examine the entrance to a large river reported to have its mouth in the south corner of Trinity Bay, having directed Mr. Tompson to follow with the cutters in two hours and stand off and on in the bay until signalled to enter.

215. A strong easterly breeze carried us quickly into the bay under sail, but it came down through the lofty gorges of Murray Prior's Range in sudden and dangerous gusts.

216. Running down the bay, a broad level low country valley opened out southerly between Murray Prior's Peaks and the Western Main Coast Range, which here approaches the coast line.

217. In the centre a bold and lofty mountain of perfect pyramidal form and of 3,016 feet elevation, rose from the centre of the lowland. I named this remarkable mountain "Walsh's Pyramid," after my friend, the Honorable W. H. Walsh (now Speaker of the Legislative Assembly of Queensland). Behind Walsh's Pyramid the broad indigo-colored bulk of Bellenden Kerr rose into the clouds. Bell's Peaks

17

Peaks opened out on the left. Three prominent mountains, of the Main Coast Range, were named after my friends, Mr. Brinsley G. Sheridan, P.M., Mr. F. Y. Williams, Commissioner of Crown Lands, and Mr. E. Whitfield, merchant, of Cardwell, to whom the expedition has been indebted for many acts of courtesy and much substantial assistance.

218. In the centre of the southern arc of the bay the broad opening of an apparently large river appeared.

219. I sounded along the banks, which appeared to fill this portion of the bay, obtaining only three feet of water over them, when the lead suddenly dropped into a broad two-fathom channel running straight in and soon deepening to three and-a-half fathoms. The cutters arrived in the bay, and followed us in with a fair fresh breeze, and anchored within the river mouth in five fathoms, these soundings extending right across from bank to bank.

220. I continued to ascend the channel, and sound ahead in the whaleboat, and having found six, seven, and eight fathoms for two miles with a breadth of half-a-mile, and no apparent diminution of breadth, we returned and brought the cutters up six miles to the centre of the third reach, and anchored in three and a-half fathoms—muddy bottom—at the junction of a smaller branch coming from the direction of Walsh's Pyramid and Bellenden Kerr, which filled the whole south end of the valley at a distance of seven and eleven miles respectively. A low bald grassy hill, green as an emerald, rose from the low land towards the base of Walsh's Pyramid.

221. Examination of the smaller south branch, by which we hoped to gain the open country towards Emerald Hill, proved it in two and a-half miles to be a narrow tortuous mangrove creek.

222. Being unable to penetrate the dense mangroves in any direction to the open country to form camp, the whole party had, for the first time, to sleep on board the cutters and whaleboat, and as it rained with heavy squalls from the S.E. all night, we thoroughly realised the utter insufficiency of our shipping accommodation—in fact, I may here remark, that the attempt to carry twenty-six people in two small cutters of ten and twelve tons, necessitating the unshipping of camp equipage, erection of tents at night, and striking and shipping camp every morning, &c., added a hundredfold to the difficulties and labors of the Expedition, while the discomfort and exposure were injurious to health, and at times trying to the cheerfulness and cordial co-operation of the various members of the party. I had, however, accepted the responsibilities of command as thus constituted, and was determined to make the best of it.

223. On the morning of Friday, the 17th of October, the whaleboat and dingy—the former with myself and Messrs. Johnstone and Hill, (Perry, sounding); the latter with Messrs. Tompson and Clarke, with Native Mounted Police troopers—examined the main branch of the inlet and a S.W. main tributary.

224. We were again and again disappointed and headed back from the back country by the dense mangrove belt. In every direction the channel of this estuary broke up and ended abruptly in mangrove swamps, at times apparently so near the forest country at the base of the ranges that roads and wharves on the deep water could doubtless be constructed with facility with granite metal and gravel from the mountains behind, should the magnificent shipping capabilities of this perfectly land-locked harbor ever require to be drawn upon for the use of an auriferous back country or coast sugar lands.

225. The latter certainly exist at a practicable distance under Bellenden Kerr and in small valleys N.W. of the Trinity Harbor, as I named this new port.

226. When returning on board we saw two parties of blacks in outrigger canoes, and endeavored to get them to fraternise; but they jumped ashore and disappeared in the mangroves and mud, abandoning their vessels.

227. On examination these proved to be beautifully formed from a trunk of a red cedar, scooped out evidently by some sharp iron instrument, and perfectly shaped outside, with good stem and stern lines, both alike, and ornamented with a thin broad protruding prow at each end,* the outrigger being attached by three sets of cross sticks in a remarkably pretty and artistic manner.

228. These little craft have great buoyancy and can stand a pretty rough sea, and doubtless were those made use of when these gentry boarded and attempted to fire and take the schooner "Will-o'-the-Wisp," at 3 a.m. one morning, off Fitzroy Island, when, according to the statement in McGillivray's "Voyage of H.M.S. 'Rattlesnake,'" they threw blazing tea-tree bark down the hatches and nearly killed the master and crew.

229. These blacks are big hulking fellows, of a lighter copper-color than we are accustomed to see to the southward, and with close curling woolly hair like Polynesians or Papuans—in fact, both here and at the Johnstone, the Native Mounted Police troopers told me that " that fellow got him hair all same like it Kanaka." It is possible that local climatic influences and abundance of certain fish, wild yams (especially the taro of the South Sea Islands), and fruits, &c., may have maintained in these people a longer adherence to the characteristics of the parent stock, whether Papuan or Polynesian, which existed long ages ago, ere Mr. Mallett's system of terrestrial subsidences left a great Pacific continent shattered into the thousand islands of a vast and deep Pacific Ocean. One is the more induced to accept such a solution of the mystery because these people, although differing in certain points, are still undoubtedly the brethren of the whole " black " race of Australia, and that in less fertile districts to the north we again found the exact counterparts of our southern aborigines.

230. Having thoroughly examined this inlet, we made sail outwards and anchored for the night close to the left bank inside the entrance in five fathoms, and formed camp on a patch of open sound ground close the beach; water was discovered about 200 yards along the beach westward, and 100 yards inland, in a native well.

231. It is impossible not to regret that the noble estuary of Trinity Harbor should not be the immediate outlet of some one of the extensive agricultural basins of this coast; that it should penetrate a purely granitic—instead of, as in those more favored localities, a schistose and volcanic—country; that its deep, spacious, and completely land-locked waters—on which fleets could ride—are so imperfectly connected with what, from the indications observed along the coast and interior north and south, may prove to be a highly auriferous back country.   232. It

---

* A peculiarity observed on this coast by Captain Cook above a century ago (vide "Cook's Voyages", vol. III., p. 649), at which time, however, he remarked that the canoes were hollowed out, "perhaps by fire"—" the outside is wholly unmarked by any tool."

232. It is impossible, however, to forecast the destiny of such a spot. No white man has ever yet penetrated the mountain region to the rear of Trinity Harbor—a region which lies eastward of Kennedy's track of 1848, and between the watershed of the rivers Tully, Murray, Macalister, Hull, Herbert, Johnstone, and Mitchell, to the south; and Hann's track but of Weary Bay, and the Palmer River Diggings, on the north—a lofty watershed region containing, next to Mount Kosciusco, and, possibly, some of his fellows of the southern Alps, the highest mountains in Australia, which shed their drainage by the before-named rivers E. and S.E. into the Pacific, and W. and N.W. into the far-distant Gulf of Carpentaria—a complete renversement of the watershed system of southern Australia, with a geological formation strongly indicative of auriferous deposits on its coast margin, and abutting northerly upon the very rich alluvial diggings and auriferous slates of the Palmer River.

233. Should such auriferous deposits be developed to the rear of Trinity Harbor, I believe very little engineering difficulty will be encountered in forming the necessary wharves on deep water, and, from the appearance of the ranges, I do not anticipate any difficulty in obtaining a passable road over them to the interior.

234. As a harbor of refuge in heavy northerly and easterly gales, Trinity Harbor, if properly surveyed, and the entrance buoyed and beaconed, will prove valuable to the rapidly increasing coasting shipping.

235. We had very little opportunity of observing the tides, but believe them to be very similar to those at Fitzroy Island, where, according to the Admiralty Chart (sheet XVI.) and Coast-sailing Directory, it is "high water, F. and C., xxh 15m; springs rise 7 to 12 feet."

236. During our two days' stay in Trinity Harbor a gale had been blowing outside from the S.E., heavy vicious rain squalls at times coming down upon us out of the dark cloud cap of Bellenden Kerr, apparently the lofty centre of atmospheric disturbance on this part of the coast.

237. At 3 a.m. of the 18th October, when at anchor at the mouth of the harbor, assisting the watch to get an awning over the boom to keep us dry during one of these heavy squalls, I unfortunately slipped on the wet deck, fell over a sharp angle of the hatch and broke a rib over the region of the heart; one of the seamen sewed a canvas band tightly round me, and it got well in a month.

238. At 9 a.m. the same day, all being on board, we sailed straight out of Trinity Harbor, carrying nothing under two fathoms on the edge of the eastern banks (there was deeper water inside of us), and on reaching three fathoms, with Double Island clear of Oak-tree Point, the N.W. sandy point of the bay with a clump of casuarina, steered direct for "Haycock Island," ten miles on a N.N.W. course.

239. Several heavy squalls from the S.S.E. and S.E. swept down upon us, between Fitzroy Island and the main land of Cape Grafton, and out of Bellenden Kerr, which seemed still to pursue us with his wrath for our neglect of him en passant. We trust, however, that clearer skies and smoother seas will enable us to make his acquaintance when no storm-rack or cloud-cap obscures his ample brow.

240. At 2 p.m. we rounded to under the N. side of Double Island, inside the anchorage recommended in the Admiralty Charts and Sailing Directions; but, finding that we were exposed to the full swing of the ocean swell setting straight in through the Trinity Opening, fifteen miles distant to the N.E., we shifted round to a snug berth between the west end of the island and the main land, two hundred yards off the peculiarly distorted schistose cliffs, which descend to a pretty openly timbered and grassy flat with smooth sandy beach very suitable for landing, where we formed camp, and made all snug afloat and ashore until the S.E. weather should moderate; as, however well the cutters might behave in such weather, the whaleboat, being too large to be taken on board of either, had to be sailed by Perry with a crew of boatmen and Native Mounted Police—thus reducing the weatherly capabilities of the Expedition to those of an open boat.

241. Suffering much pain in moving from the broken rib, with difficulty of breathing, I camped on shore for a few days to enable the bone to knit and pain to abate, and permit of my attending to my duties, and to the safety of the Expedition committed to my charge.

242. Sunday, the 19th, was kept as a day of rest, but I was unfortunately too ill to be able to read service.

243. As water was required in camp I despatched Mr. Tompson in charge of a party in the whale-boat and dingy, on Monday morning, the 20th of October, to land on the mainland, opposite where were the smokes of blacks' camps, and where doubtless a supply would be obtained.

244. From the approach of the Main Coast Range to the sea at Trinity Harbor it rapidly assumes a more lofty wall-like structure, and opposite Double Island and thence N.W. rises sheer up from behind the beach to the height of four mountains—Mount Garioch of 2,189 feet, Mount Mar of 2,214 feet, Mount Formantine of 2,612 feet, and Mount Buchan of 2,086 feet—named after the four districts of my native county, Aberdeenshire; the whole receiving the name "Macalister's Range," after the Honorable Arthur Macalister, now Colonial Secretary and Premier of Queensland.

245. Mr. Johnstone and his troopers, and Mr. Hill, accompanied Mr. Tompson, and I requested them to ascend Macalister's Range, obtain a correct idea of the direction of the back country drainage, and procure specimens of the rocks of the neighborhood.

246. The shore party returned on board in the afternoon with a plentiful supply of good water, obtained from a narrow lagoon nearly two miles long, running parallel to and only divided from the sea by the high sandy beach on which a number of blacks' camps were situated.

247. Immediately after landing a considerable mob of blacks came out of their camps, and in the most daring manner attempted to prevent Mr. Johnstone's advance. According to his instructions Mr. Johnstone did not allow a shot to be fired, but this only appeared to add to their insolence and daring, as they advanced to within thirty yards, shipped their spears in the woomeras and poised them to throw; then, and not till then, the sniders opened upon them, but still they appeared utterly reckless as to the results, and their leader, a big hulking ferocious looking savage of over six feet in height, with several of his more daring followers, tried still to throw their spears, and to induce the rest to come on when severely wounded.

248. From the discoveries made in their camps we all heartily rejoiced at the severe lesson which their unwarrantable hostility had brought upon them, and that such blood-thirsty bullying scoundrels had at length met more than their match; for undoubtedly had the shore party been a poor shipwrecked crew cast ashore from the Pacific Ocean, as many hundreds of poor fellows have been, who have never been heard of more, not one would have escaped the certain destruction and mutilation which is almost invariable in such cases.

249. In

19

249. In every camp along the beach for two miles unmistakable evidences of wholesale habitual cannibalism were discovered; heaps of human bones and skulls were found in each camp, and in some, roasted and partially eaten bodies were found beside the fires at which they had been cooked. Lumps of half-eaten human flesh were found in the gins' dilly bags.

250. These people resemble those in Trinity Harbor, and are doubtless part of the same tribe. They are of most ferocious expression of countenance, and are large and powerful men. It is to be hoped, therefore, viewing the now rapid increase of settlement and commerce along this coast, that masters of vessels and others will give them a wide berth, and in no way run risks with them that have brought disaster even among quieter tribes.

251. The shore party ascended Macalister's Range, and had a magnificent view of the coast north and south; but, inland, ranges beyond ranges in wild confusion presented a labyrinth of valleys, the watersheds of which could not be determined.

252. Quartz-reef outcrops were found upon Macalister's Range, the general formation being granite and some slate. Canoes similar to those at Trinity Harbor were found in the fresh-water lagoon behind the beach—one of which was forty feet long, cut out of one log of red cedar.

253. The strata of which Double Island is composed have been uptilted and contorted, forming a sharp razor-back ridge, steep towards the W., N., and E., on which sides the stratification of white stratified sandstone, quartz, slate (allied to the Brisbane slates), and micaceous schist are very clearly exposed.

254. On Thursday, the 23rd of October, camp was struck, all were on board by 7·45 a.m., and the cutters under weigh for Snapper Island, twenty-nine miles N.N.W., with a fresh S.S.E. breeze.

255. Macalister's Range rose in an unbroken wall from the sea, in no place receding more than two miles from the shore until its termination in Mount Garioch, in latitude 16° 36′ 30″ S.

256. Behind its northern extremity, a lofty peak of 3,573 feet, which I named "Harris' Peak," after my friend the Honorable George Harris, M.L.C., appears to belong to a more distant lateral range.

257. At Mount Garioch, the granitic formation again appears to give place to the schistose, which in a lower range—also parallel to and close to the coast, which I named the "Heights of Victory"—in eleven miles ends in a pretty jungle-clad hill, with openly-timbered summit, named "Mount Beaufort," four and a-half miles W.N.W. of Island Point—the origin of the latter name being evident from the apparent isolation of the headland before the low land connecting it with the coast rises into view.

258. In running down from Island Point to Snapper Island, past the "Low Islands" (low coral reefs with sand and mud, clothed with mangroves and low scrub), I was much struck with the evident occurrence of another great coast basin of rich land in a renewal of schistose country, as well as with the grandeur of the mountain background, of which I had never previously heard of or read any reference whatever.

259. In very carefully examining the coast line with the opera-glass, I observed the opening of a river under Mount Beaufort, and of a more important one in the N.W. corner of Trinity Bay, about two and a-half to three miles W. of Snapper Island.

260. Low ranges of jungle-clad heights rose from the shore line between these two rivers in continuation of the "Heights of Victory"—so named because I had ultimately the gratification of proving that my theories of the coast formation were correct, and those of others with whom I had conversed on the subject, and who were strongly of opinion that no good land would be obtained N. of Cape Grafton, were in error. I named the jungle-clad hills the "Heights of Dagmar," and a higher series running back to meet them from behind Snapper Island, the "Heights of Alexandra."

261. Behind the Heights of Victory and Dagmar—as at Bellenden Kerr, and divided from them by similar apparently jungle-clad valleys—rose a vast range of rugged mountains densely wooded to the summits, which now and then exposed their crenelated peaks, precipices, and rocky pinnacles through rifts in the cloud-banks, which rested day and night upon their lofty shoulders.

262. This mountain range appears to be nearly, if not quite as high as Bellenden Kerr, and about twenty-five miles in length—its N.W. extremity sinking down into a deep and broad valley, running in the direction of the new Palmer River diggings. I named this range after the Honorable A. H. Palmer, the late Colonial Secretary of Queensland.

263. To the N. of this range, and of the broad valley which is apparently that of the new river inside Snapper Island, the mountains again rise into lofty granite peaks of most picturesque outline, and of nearly 4,000 feet elevation. Of these, Thornton's Peaks, behind the N.W. end of the "Heights of Alexandra," is most conspicuous from the southward, hiding "Peter Botte," of 3,311 feet, until Snapper Island is passed, going northerly.

264. At 2·45 p.m., we anchored under the W. end of Snapper Island, three boats' lengths off the usual sand-spit, in six fathoms, sand; "Black Rock" on with the highest point of Cape Tribulation. A heavy swell rolled in from the eastward, but the weather was fine, with a fresh breeze from E.S.E. At 3 p.m., the thermometer stood at 82° in the shade. Clouds lay along the highest mountain tops of the mainland. The aneroid barometer registered 30·0.

265. The great anxiety which I felt not to fail in meeting Mr. Sedheim at the Endeavour mouth on the first of November, as arranged before our departure from Cardwell, so as to open communication with the Palmer River, and enable the diggers there to be speedily relieved, and dray-road communication established before the possible "rush" of a large population, obliged me to defer the exploration of the interesting coast line opposite our anchorage until the return voyage, and, with the sanction of the Government, to proceed at once to the Endeavour, as, with our small vessels and large party, a series of strong northerly winds might protect our arrival there, and mar the beneficial arrangements which had been initiated for the relief of the enterprising prospectors of the new gold field.

THE ENDEAVOUR RIVER.

266. At 6 a.m. on Friday, the 24th of October, all were on board, and the cutters standing northwards for the Endeavour River, with a moderate S.E. breeze on a course N.¼E.

267. Inside Snapper Island the bold rocky headland of the mainland, which forms the northern extremity of Trinity Bay and will doubtless be hereafter a leading point for observations in making the entrance

20

entrances of the new rivers close by, has no name. I therefore beg to suggest the expediency of requesting the Lords Commissioners of the Admiralty to name it "Cape Kimberley," in honor of Her Majesty's late Secretary of State for the Colonies.

268. From Cape Kimberley to Cape Tribulation the ranges rise, densely-wooded to the summits, from small basins of rich jungle lands along the coast. There appears to be abundance of fresh water. The formation of Snapper Island and of those coast mountains is granitic and schistose, and the lofty terrace-like slopes of flat mountain present a succession of fine sites for coffee plantations. Some of the coast basins are evidently suitable for sugar.

269. At 9 a.m. Cape Tribulation was abeam, the breeze freshening from the S. with a confused cross sea, caused by several openings in the Great Barrier reefs, five or six miles eastward.

270. The well-wooded country south of Cape Tribulation, of this eventful portion of Captain Cook's voyage, 104 years ago, again changed to rugged granitic ranges round Weary Bay, which was passed at noon, the opening of Captain (afterward Admiral) King's Bloomfield Rivulet being visible within a grey rocky headland, backed by rugged hills, steep and, according to Hann's report, impracticable for dray traffic.*

271. Lofty and steep rocky mountains continued to rise abruptly from the coast, nearly as far as Walker Point, the general coloring having changed from the dark green of rich vegetation which characterises the country of the Johnstone, Bellenden Kerr, and Arthur Palmer's ranges, to the usual light dirty brownish green of the Australian coast.

272. Captain Cook's Hope Islands were passed on the starboard beam. Their name commemorates the only ray of hope of escape from a watery grave which cheered the gallant explorers and navigators in H.M.S. "Endeavour," when she lay grazing on the coral of Endeavour Reef, visible four and a-half miles N.E. of us, and whence she escaped, as by a miracle, to be hove down for repairs in that Endeavour River which was our own present destination.

273. From the north end of the rocky range, in 15° 46' S., lower scrub-clad hills, with open grassy brows and valleys towards the ocean, extended to Walker Point and thence fell back westward, forming the southern watershed of the Annan and Esk rivers of the Admiralty charts.

274. "Monkhouse Point" rose abruptly from the sea in a rocky headland of granite boulders, five miles N.N.W. of Walker Point; and behind the former Mount Cook, clothed with dense stunted scrub to his dome-shaped summit, rose to an elevation of 1,476 feet, marking the position of the Endeavour River beyond it.

275. North and west of Walker Point the high coast ranges fall suddenly away; the face of the country completely changes; for, although the rugged granitic formation still faces the ocean north of the Annan and Esk estuary, in the narrow coast range of Mount Cook to Endeavour mouth, inland, a level sandstone country, broken by isolated flat-topped sandstone mountains, stretches far to the west in the direction of the Palmer River diggings, and, as we rapidly opened the estuary of the Endeavour, a high coast range of similar flat-topped hills, with red sandstone escarpments, stretched thirteen miles N.N.E. along the shore to Cape Bedford.

276. At 4.30 p.m. we ran in with a strong south-easter under the steep high land of "Grassy Hill," and dropped our anchors inside the Endeavour River, in four fathoms, sandy bottom, close to the spot described in "Cook's Voyages," Vol. III., p. 557, as the site of his shore camp and disembarkation of stores, previous to heaving the "Endeavour" down. Our camp was formed on shore about the same place.

277. The best description of the Endeavour River extant, even now, since its settlement as a seaport town under the name of its discoverer, a century ago (Cooktown), is undoubtedly that written by the gallant navigator himself in the above-mentioned volume. Accurate in every detail, even after such a lapse of time, every physical feature of the harbor and river is correctly described, and even the character of the aborigines appears to have no more changed than have apparently the form of their canoes, spears, and woomeras. It is noteworthy that here Captain Cook learned the native name "Kangaroo," for that marsupial, which was here seen and described for the first time by Mr. (afterwards Sir Joseph) Banks.

278. From the "Grassy Hill," which rises steep from the landing, the broad valley of the river was seen to come from between high flat-topped sandstone ranges to the N.W. Three of these ranges extend along the western end of the valley, having bluff ends and perpendicular escarpments. At the south end of the more southerly one a valley runs in a W.S.W. direction, and, leaving another similar but more distinct range to the southward, presented an admirable exit from the Endeavour Valley to the Palmer River diggings, and by this route we fully expected Mr. Selheim would arrive, having completed a marked-tree line from the new diggings.

279. It blew a gale from the S.E., moderating in the morning. When the morning watch was called on board the "Flying Fish," it was found that she had sprung a leak and there were two feet of water in the hold. The hands were at once set to work removing the cargo, stores, &c., but unfortunately a considerable number of things were damaged. The stores, &c., were all landed from the cutter, preparatory to her being hove down for repairs, at the spot where H.M.S. "Endeavour" had gone through similar treatment.

280. At 11.30 a.m. on Saturday, the 25th of October, the camp being busily engaged drying stores, pitching more tents, cleaning fire-arms, &c., &c., we were all startled by the sudden appearance of the tall masts and yards of a large steamer over the mangrove belt towards the point, which she rapidly passed, and inside of which she brought up and made fast to the shore where Captain Cook first moored the "Endeavour."

281. We soon learned that this new and unexpected arrival was the A.S.N. Co's. fine steamer "Leichhardt," with a complete Government staff of police—to be stationed at the Endeavour—of Gold Fields' Department, for the new diggings, in charge of Mr. Howard St. George, Gold Commissioner, and of Engineer of Roads, under the able leadership of the indefatigable head of that department for the northern districts, Mr. A. C. MacMillan, charged on this occasion with the responsible duty of finding and making a road to the diggings. Some seventy hardy miners accompanied them, the expedition being under the immediate charge of Lieut. Connor, R.N., of H.M. surveying schooner "Pearl," who at once commenced a survey of the estuary and entrance.

282. The

* Report from Mr. William Hann, leader of the Northern Expedition, page 11.

282. The official correspondence by this opportunity informed me that since my departure from the settlements the continued good reports from the Palmer diggings, and the imminence of an immediate "rush," calculated greatly to magnify the distress and danger which it had been part of the duty of my expedition, co-operating with Mr. Selheim, to make provision for, had called forth immediate Executive action to provide for all possible emergencies.

283. On the day before (Friday) we had sailed into a silent, lonely, distant river mouth, with thoughts going back a century to the arrival of the brave navigator, its discoverer and his people, in knee breeches, three-cornered hats, and small swords, pigtails, and silver shoe-buckles. On Saturday we were in the middle of a phase of enterprise peculiarly characteristic of the present day—of a young diggings' township—men hurrying to and fro, tents rising in all directions, horses grazing, and neighing for their mates, all round us—the shouts of sailors and laborers landing more horses and cargo, combined with the rattling of the donkey engine, cranes, and chains—many familiar faces of old friends, thought to be hundreds of miles distant, peeped in at our tent doors for a morning call, or bade us welcome to the spacious decks of the "Leichhardt," where we received the greatest hospitality and courtesy from Captain Saunders and his officers.

284. On Monday, the 27th of October, the "Flying Fish" was laid on the bank at the south side of the harbor for repairs, when it was found that a hole had opened in the seam of the planking of the port bilge, which was soon put to rights, and the rest of the bottom overhauled.

285. On Tuesday, the 28th of October, I started in the whaleboat, accompanied by Mr. Johnstone and crew of Native Mounted Police the Botanist, and Perry taking soundings, and we went up the Endeavour River to examine its banks for agricultural lands.

286. We went ten miles up the river, finding the soundings to correspond with the chart, but were disappointed in our search for good soils, except in one place at our highest point of ascent, where a small plain on the south bank, with surrounding open forest, showed a rich soil of some five hundred acres in extent. This is evidently the spot discovered by Sir Joseph Banks, and described in "Captain Cook's Voyages," Vol. III., page 569.

287. A deep creek entered the river on the east side of this small plain, with a low, stony hill on its eastern or right bank, previously seen from our camp. We landed on that bank of the creek, and ascended the hill, which was composed of slate allied to the Brisbane slates.

288. As we ascended the north side of the hill from the boat, Mr. Macmillan, leaving his horses below, climbed the south side, and we had a pleasant meeting on the summit, neither party having been aware at starting of the proposed destination of the others.

289. From the summit of this hill a comprehensive view of the valleys of the Endeavour, Annan, and Esk rivers were obtained from their mouths till lost in the N.W. and S.W. ranges respectively. West of our stand-point the two nearer lofty, flat-topped, sandstone ranges were distant only some six miles, and the south-west, and more distant one, previously mentioned, was distinctly visible; the gap which I had previously seen from the mouth of the Endeavour here presenting a most inviting outlet towards the Palmer.

290. With the exception of the small plain below us to the westward, and its surrounding area of forest, not an acre of good land was to be seen within the range of vision. Even as pastoral country the region around us had not a single attractive feature, but appeared like the fallen-in wreck of a great primeval sandy desert plain clothed with coarse grasses and stunted, dirty green, open forest; the scattered, flat-topped ranges, all of the same height, remaining as standing monuments of the ruin wrought by "degradation" and "abrasion."

291. Having fortified the inner man at our dinner camp on the creek with Tooth's preserved Clifton mutton, Mr. MacMillan started through the S.W. Gap to explore ahead for a passage to the westward, carrying with him our best wishes for success, and we turned our boat's head down the river, and returned to camp at 6.30 p.m.

292. I regretted being unable to recommend the channel of the Endeavour up to this point for light draught vessels, from the fact that it heads away from the direct route inland, which starts from the wharves at Cooktown direct for the interior, on a line five or six miles to the southward.

293. The "Flying Fish" was again floated this afternoon, brought to the anchorage of our camp, and reshipped her stores from the cutter "Coquette."

294. On Wednesday, the 29th of October, Captain Saunders, understanding that I proposed to examine the Annan and Esk rivers, most courteously volunteered to take us round in the fine screw launch "Swift," of the A.S.N. Co., sent up as tender to the s.s. "Leichhardt." We accordingly started at 9 a.m. on board the diminutive steamer, with whaleboat and usual crew in tow, which quickly ran us round under the rocky bluffs and headlands outside Grassy Hill, Mount Cook, and Monkhouse Point into the broad, shallow bay between the latter and Walker's Point.

295. Captain Saunders ran down the three-fathom line towards the N.W. beach till the entrance of the Annan opened southwards, through white sandbanks, now, at young flood, showing six feet above water, where he anchored in one fathom till I should have sounded the entrance in the whaleboat.

296. At this time of tide the water was shallow right across, shoaling to three feet on the bar; but the tide making in half an hour, we steamed right in with nearly four feet, deepening close to the steep east fronting banks to two fathoms, and shoaling again within to six feet on a southerly course.

297. Within the outer banks the channel made a sharp turn west and then north-west, round a steep and long sand-spit, and opened a fine reach of the river about a mile long.

298. A moderately-sized mangrove creek, blocked up with sandbanks, entered on the south bank opposite the entrance, corresponding with the position of the Esk.

299. Half way up the Annan reach we grounded on sand banks, which here block the river; but the tide rising, we succeeded in ascending another mile, where we landed to examine the country.

300. The soil was found to be a poor sandy clay loam on a substratum of rotten sandstone rock and whitish pipe-clay, and clothed with coarse-bladed grass, white-stemmed poplar gum-trees, and some bloodwood. On the south bank, a narrow belt of jungle, a few yards through, fronted country of the same worthless description.

301. The view up the river, W.S.W., bordered on the right bank by the above narrow jungle, with the view of the S.W. ranges, was very pleasing. The sharp point of St. George's Peak, named by Mr. Macmillan, and ascended by him and Mr. Gold Commissioner St. George, was about two miles to the N.W.

302. I regret that neither the river nor its surrounding country can be recommended for agricultural or commercial purposes, unless the new diggings on the seaward side of the ranges—lately reported by Mr. Douglas, of the Native Mounted Police—extend down this valley, when the Annan may become a means of carriage with very light draft vessels. Some better land, a few hundreds of acres in extent, was seen from the hills some distance up the river, but did not offer sufficient inducements to me to lose valuable time in examining it closely, as we had the prospect of exploring and discovering not hundreds but many thousands of acres of far richer lands to the southward; we, therefore, returned to camp at 6 p.m.

303. Mr. Macmillan kindly supplied us with several dray-loads of water from the spring—a mile distant—with which the cutters filled up their watercasks.

304. Water was found in several places on the sea side of Mount Cook and Grassy Hill, and in a small spring behind the camp, but the main supply was obtained from the small creek about a mile to the south. Water is also reported in the Sailing Directory, and in the voyages of Captain Cook and of H.M.S. "Rattlesnake," about a mile along the sandy beach on the north side of the mouth of the river; but, from the numbers of blacks' camps scattered about the country on that side, I presume there must be water over the whole locality.

305. By letter from the Honorable the Colonial Secretary, of date the 13th of October, I received advice that—in case I found it advisable to take advantage of it—it had been arranged with the A.S.N. Co. that the charter of the "Leichhardt" should embrace free passages to any or all of my party back to Cardwell.

306. Five weeks' experience of the cutters "Flying Fish" and "Coquette"—of the great loss of time and inconvenience caused by the necessity of forming camp ashore in some sheltered anchorage, not to be found every day without derangement of plans and curtailment of distances travelled, with corresponding serious loss of time, not to mention the additional labor to the hands, especially the Native Mounted Police troopers, in breaking up and pitching camp, landing and shipping the whole camp equipage, &c., by the boats daily, combined with great exposure to sun and weather, and confined and cramped position when on board, had convinced me, ere my arrival at the Endeavour River, that the general results of the Expedition were being seriously interfered with by these small vessels, even with the fair trade winds with which we had been hitherto favored. Now, the prevalence of strong south-easters, blowing, at times, half a gale, dead ahead (on a S.E. course), without any appearance of abatement and with a nasty jumping cross sea, convinced me that it would be extremely imprudent to attempt to beat south against it, it being impossible to beat up from one safe anchorage to another any day between daylight and dark, and with no means beyond an old nail can of cooking for so large a party on board; and that the sooner the cutters were got rid of and replaced by a vessel of sufficient capacity the better.

307. Such a vessel—the schooner "Flirt," of 34 tons register—I believed to be at that time in Cardwell, and open for charter (the necessity was also forced upon me of re-organising my party on a different footing (vide my despatches of the 30th of October, 1872). I therefore determined to ship the whole Expedition on board the s.s. "Leichhardt," land and camp them on No. II. South Barnard Island, thirty-two miles N. of Cardwell, and opposite a portion of the coast from Clump Point to Double Point, which I wished to explore, thus preventing loss of time or the possibility of the party being left in a state of enforced idleness, and to proceed to Cardwell to communicate with the Government by wire, and make the arrangements required by these necessary changes.

308. My reasons for selecting No. II. South Barnard Island for a camp were strong ones, viz.: That it was strongly recommended to me by my second officer, Mr. Sub-Inspector Johnstone, for that purpose, having plenty of good water, wood, oysters, fish, pigeons, and scrub hens; that it was a healthy open camp; that by having game and fish a salutary change of food would be obtained for my party, and considerable economy in rations secured; that it was handy to Cardwell, and, as above stated, close to and opposite a coast to be explored; and, above all, that it placed us again to windward of our work, which would thus be thoroughly under command, and therefore more rapidly and perfectly completed.

309. On Thursday, the 30th of October, the Expedition party and stores—with the exception of the heavy rations of flour and sugar, left in the cutters—were all shipped on board the "Leichhardt," the whaleboat and dingy where hoisted to the davits, and the masters of the cutters received instructions to make sail at once for the South Barnard Island camp, and there report themselves to the officer in charge.

310. At 6 a.m. on Friday, the 31st of October, the "Leichhardt" steamed out of the Endeavour, leaving a lively little seaport under her starboard quarter, gleaming with white tents, and noisily busy with workmen, where, a week before, we had found a silent wilderness.

311. The first destination of the s.s. "Leichhardt" was the "Three Isles" or "Low Isles," twenty-four miles N.N.E. of Cooktown, and nine miles N.E. of Cape Bedford, for the purpose of shipping some twenty tons of bêche-de-mer, cured at a fishing station on one of these small islands.

312. Steaming rapidly along the land, the same high, flat-topped sandstone ranges rose all along the coast out to Cape Bedford, their red and lofty escarpments showing the apparent entrances of caves which I much regretted being unable, on this occasion, to land and examine. I named the second high hill of this range from the river "Mount Saunders," in recognition of the courtesy and assistance received from that gentleman.

313. The whole appearance of this district indicates the existence of coal and fossils. Mr. MacMillan has since found both on his route to the Palmer. The quality of the coal I have not yet learned, but the fossils Mr. Staiger tells me belong to Daintree's "Desert sandstone," or "conglomerate," of which similar flat-topped ranges extend over an area of country some fifty miles square around Gilberton, where I have been Gold Commissioner since October, 1871. These specimens would form an interesting addition to the rock specimens collected by us along the N.E. coast, and now in the Brisbane Museum. They only number about one hundred, but will form a nucleus to a collection of the coast formations which, added to by successive explorers, may prove a useful link in determining the geological structure of the whole Cape York Peninsula, and the rich gold fields at its base.

314. The fact of Mr. MacMillan's fossils proving an identity of formation with the Desert sandstones of the Gilbert Ranges, is in itself most interesting, and goes far to show the primeval existence of a vast sandstone tableland, as before remarked, recumbent upon the auriferous slates,

quartz

23

quartz, elvanitez, granites, metamorphic mica schists, and porphyry of Northern Queensland, extending from the watershed of the Flinders and Gilbert rivers, to Capes Bedford and Melville, probably originally over the whole of Northern Queensland, in one unbroken dreary plain; and these regions having been subsequently prepared for the great designs of the present earthly "dispensation" in which we live by the "subsidence" and anterior—almost entire—disappearance of the great sandstone plateau by "denudation," the underlying strata being, according to Malsitt's system, distorted by the very forces called into existence by that subsidence, both igneous and by lateral pressure, and made ready for the enterprise of man, now rushing headlong, pick and shovel in hand, to exhume their long-hidden treasures.

315. At 9 a.m. of the 31st of October, the "Leichhardt" anchored on the N.W. side of the "Three Isles," and during the day the shipment of bêche-de-mer in small gunny bags was completed. Some enormous "clam shells" were brought off, and abundance of sponge, which is also plentiful on the adjacent reefs of the "Great Barrier," whence the bêche-de-mer is brought in small vessels to the island, where it is prepared by a process beginning with scalding in hot water, and drying in a closed house with mangrove wood smoke, and much turning, requiring considerable attention and care.

316. There are a few Europeans on the island, but most of the employees are Kanakas—healthy, happy-looking, and fat.

317. The "Leichhardt" got under weigh at 4 a.m. on Saturday, the 1st of November, at 7 a.m. passed the mouth of the Endeavour, and sighted H.M. schooner "Beagle" at anchor off the entrance, and the cutters "Flying Fish" and "Coquette" beating out of the estuary, and at 8·30 a.m. S. of Walker Point, the brigantine "Margaret Chessel" and a small cutter bound N. Double Island was passed at 3 p.m., and at 8 p.m. we brought up for the night under High Island of the Frankland Group, N. side quarter of a mile off shore.

318. From the high bridge of the "Leichhardt" I enjoyed a better prospect of the coast line from Snapper Island to Bellenden Kerr than it had been possible to obtain from the cutters, and was still more firmly convinced of the existence of good rivers and large areas of agricultural country inside Cape Kimberley, and around Bellenden Kerr mountains.

319. At 6 a.m. on the 2nd of November, the "Leichhardt" steamed away south, past the now to us familiar coast, the Johnstone, Mourilyan Harbor, No. IV. N. Barnard, and at 10 a.m. brought up quarter of a mile off the N.W. side of No. II. South Barnard Island.

320. The expedition party was landed in charge of Mr. Johnstone; with whom I left full instructions for the exploration of the coast, and the despatch of the cutter "Coquette" to Cardwell on her arrival, to communicate with me, and at once went on in the "Leichhardt" to arrange the contemplated necessary changes.

321. We arrived at Cardwell at 4 p.m., when I immediately communicated with the Honorable the Colonial Secretary by wire, and finding, as I anticipated, that the schooner "Flirt" was lying alongside the jetty and open to charter, I telegraphed for permission to charter her and to discharge the cutters, which was promptly granted.

322. On Friday, November 7th, the cutter "Coquette" arrived with despatches from camp, "all well," and coast being explored as directed. The cutters had been six days and nights beating down the coast from the Endeavour, a circumstance which confirmed me in my opinion that the course adopted had been in every way the most judicious under the circumstances.

323. On Saturday, the 8th of November, a charter of the schooner "Flirt" was completed with Mr. Charles Tighe, of Newcastle, New South Wales, part owner, and I despatched the "Coquette" to Barnard Island Camp to recall the "Flying Fish," which arrived on the 11th of November, and was paid off, transhipping stores, &c., into the schooner "Flirt" alongside the jetty.

324. At 3 p.m. on the same day, I went on board, and, accompanied by my friend Brinsley G. Sheridan, P.M., Cardwell, hauled out from the jetty and anchored, awaiting telegrams from Brisbane, and the arrival of the "Bunyip" with despatches from the Government, which arrived on Thursday, at 10 a.m.

325. Owing to interruptions to the south on the telegraph line, communication was not opened till the evening of the 13th, and I awaited replies to telegrams to the Honorable the Colonial Secretary, till the morning of Friday, the 14th of November.

THE RIVERS MULGRAVE AND RUSSELL.

326. At 5 a.m. on Friday, the 14th of November, the schooner "Flirt" stood out of Port Hinchinbrook for Dunk Island, to which Mr. Johnstone had shifted camp a few days before, with a light westerly breeze; a dense fog caused by the smokes of the blacks' bush fires, driven seaward by the land wind, obscuring everything.

327. Towards the afternoon the breeze freshened and came dead ahead, and at 6·30 p.m. we beat up to an anchorage alongside the "Coquette," close under the S. side of the W. sand-spit of Dunk Island, in one-quarter less three fathoms sand. Mr. Johnstone and Mr. Hill came on board and reported all well.

328. On Saturday, the 15th of November, filled up with water from the watering place springs, mentioned in clause 18 of this Report; the "Coquette" came alongside and transhipped her stores, &c., and all was got ready for sailing on Monday morning.

329. Service was read on the deck of the "Flirt" at 11 a.m. on Sunday, the 16th of November. The mornings at present were calm and sultry, the heavy smoke fogs hanging low over land and sea, which the mid-day sea breeze was unable afterwards to dispel.

330. At 7 a.m. on Monday, the 17th of November, camp was broken up, and all on board the "Flirt," and we stood away N. ½ E. for the Frankland Islands with a light land breeze, the heavy smokes still obscuring the mountains of the mainland.

331. The "Coquette" returned to Cardwell to be discharged, having on board Mr. Brinsley G. Sheridan, the Police Magistrate, who had accompanied me so far in the "Flirt," Mr. Sub-Inspector F. M. Thompson, and Trooper Billy, the latter suffering from the effects of severe attacks of fever, and sent back to camp, by this opportunity, invalided.

332. The re-organised expedition was now as follows:—

1st. Officer in charge, G. Elphinstone Dalrymple.
2nd. Officer, second in charge, Mr. Sub-Inspector R. Johnstone.
3rd. Botanist, Mr. Walter Hill.   4th. Owner

4th. Owner of schooner " Flirt," Mr. Charles Tighe.
5th. Master of ditto, Mr. Henry Hall.
6th. Seaman of ditto, Arthur Lane.
7th. Ditto   ditto, Samuel Riley.
8th. Acting storekeeper and boatman, John Vickers.
9th. Boatman in charge of whaleboat, John Perry.
10th. Cook and steward (gold fields' trooper), Chas. Maidman.
10 Native Mounted Police troopers.

20

Total, twenty (20) souls; showing a saving of pay of one officer and one boatman, and rations of six men; against which had to be taken into account an excess of £5 per month on the charter party of the " Flirt," which was £80 per month *versus* £75 per month formerly paid for the cutters.

333. At 6·30 p.m. the anchor was let go in four fathoms, sandy bottom, close to the N.W. corner of No. 11. Frankland Island, referred to in clause 192 of this Report; and now the comfort and convenience of a large vessel, and absence of all necessity to camp on shore, were fully realized.

334. A nearer view of this long low island proved the correctness of McGillivray's description, viz., that it is composed of a recent coral conglomerate, *in situ* on the beach, the island being scattered over with flat blocks of the same. The low hill at either end being schistose; the island covered with low scrub.

335. The remains of an old bêche-de-mer fishing and curing station were found on its north end.

336. At 6 a.m., on the 18th of November, we were under weigh, and standing in with a light southerly breeze towards the mouth of the river, previously observed and mentioned under clause 189 of this Report as coming out through the low land under the centre of Bellenden Kerr mountains.

337. At 8·30 a.m. we brought up off the bar, having the next rocky point of the main land northerly, which I named Palmer's Point, on with the top of Great Hill; and accompanied by Mr. Johnstone, Mr. Hill, Perry, and crew of Native Mounted Police, I sounded into the river in the whaleboat.

338. Reference to the Admiralty chart (sheet XVL) shows a blunt wedge-shaped bank extending seawards from the mouth of the river, which is in latitude 17° 14′ S., longitude 145° 59′ 30″ E. This bank forces the channel over towards the N.W. shore.

339. We steered into this channel through an opening in the outer banks, on a line bringing the high peak of Mount Massie directly over Sophia's Peak; the latter being the most northerly prominence on the N. spur of Bellenden Kerr. There were only three feet on the bar at dead low-water springs.

340. Inside the banks, the peak of Mount Bartle Frere showed in the centre of the cut of the skylines of the S. spur of Bellenden Kerr, over the N. spur of Graham's Range,* for which we steered, deepening the water to six and nine feet, and between Flirt Point, the north point of the river entrance, and Point Constantine, a long sandy point clothed with grass and casuarina, forming the other head, and facing the true course of the river. About three-quarters of a mile in we obtained four and five fathoms.

341. A large basin of deep water here, completely sheltered by Point Constantine, affords safe anchorage for a considerable amount of shipping, with natural wharfage along the inside of Point Constantine and Flirt Point.

342. Opening Flirt Point, the river presented a fine reach a mile and a-half long and as broad as the Brisbane above Newstead, coming from the W.S.W. Mangroves lined the shores, backed by dense jungles, clothing the gentle slopes of Malbon Thompson's Range on the right, and the steeper Graham's Range on the left or south side.

343. We carried soundings from two fathoms to three and a-half fathoms to the head of the reach, where a fine sheet of water, formed by the junction of N. and S. branches, spreads out in the form of the letter T.

344. The scenery at this junction is beautiful and imposing. Facing the main reach which we had just ascended, the great mountain mass of Bellenden Kerr rises from the sea level to its full elevation, his base and lower spurs and glens clothed with dense jungles; his sides with thick scrubs to the summit. A lofty granite cliff is conspicuous close under his central highest peak.

345. We were now behind Malbon Thompson's and Graham's coast ranges, which, running N. and S. parallel to the coasts and to Bellenden Kerr, form, with the latter, long N. and S. valleys, drained by the two branches of this beautiful river, which I did myself the honor to name the "Mulgrave," the south branch receiving the name of the "Russell," which we ascended for about eight miles in a southerly direction.

346. This fine valley, which I named the "Vale of Mulgrave," averages four miles in breadth from range to range. On the S. it runs out without a break into that of the Johnstone—distant sixteen miles—and N. towards Trinity Harbor, distant seventeen miles. With the exception of a limited extent of mangrove flats in the lowest level of drainage opposite the junction, and between it and the base of Bellenden Kerr, the valley is full of dense jungles, similar to those upon the Johnstone, and appears to be a northern extension of that fine alluvial district.

347. From the junction the lofty peak of Mount Bartle Frere rose over the long S.W. spurs of Bellenden Kerr N. 23½° S.W. Up the N. branch of the Vale of Mulgrave, Walsh's Pyramid, an imposing bare granitic peak of 3,016 feet elevation, and of perfect pyramidal form, rises abruptly from the low lands between Bellenden Kerr and Trinity Harbor, and forms a conspicuous land mark.

348. I determined to bring the schooner in and anchor her at the junction, as a suitable place whence to complete the exploration of both branches of the river; but on our return on board, the ebb tide set out too strongly against us to allow of our doing so on the 18th, and our position off the bar being a very exposed one, the "Flirt" returned and anchored under the N. end of No. 11. Frankland Island, close to last night's anchorage, but more exposed to a heavy easterly roll, by which our night's rest

---

* *Vide* Appendix.

rest was made extremely uncomfortable. I should certainly recommend to others the anchorage close under the western sandy beach, in four fathoms, where a vessel is sheltered by the whole length of the reefs and rocky isles as far as Cocoanut Point.

349. On Wednesday, the 19th of November, we were under weigh at 6 a.m.; but a fresh land breeze headed us back from the Mulgrave towards "High Island," where it left us, and we were becalmed the whole day until too late to cross the Mulgrave Bar with daylight; we therefore anchored on the N.N.W. side of the island, in five fathoms, 400 yards from the beach.

350. High Island rises from a rocky shore of granite, alternating with schists, in beautifully-wooded acclivities, to a peak of some 400 feet elevation. On its west side is a pretty sandy beach, shaded at the base of the hill by spreading fig-trees, &c. An extensive coral reef, dry at low water, extends off the W. and S. shores, and shoals the water inside our anchorage along the beach.

351. We discovered a dangerous rock about half-a-mile off the N.E. headland of the island. When first seen it had a considerable white break over it, and afterwards showed as a small brown lump, four feet above low water. Since then I have looked for it at high water without success, although it was blowing fresh. In approaching or leaving the anchorage under the N. side of the island, vessels will require to give the N.E. headland a wide berth.

352. When becalmed off this rock, at 9 a.m., the A.S.N. Co.'s ss. "Bunyip" passed us, bound south, from the Endeavour. I sent Mr. Johnstone on board to request the captain to report us all well, and forwarded a letter to Mr. Sheridan, P.M., Cardwell, requesting him to telegraph the discovery of the above rock to the Portmaster, Captain G. P. Heath, R.N., the trade along this coast being rapidly on the increase, and the above danger very near the usual course of vessels.

353. The formation of High Island is granite, schist, quartz, hornblende, and mica; tourmalin was found on the N. headland, and quartz with mica.

354. Several small streams of excellent water were found on the island, descending its N., N.E., and S.E. sides. They are evidently permanent, and, being close to the beach, are serviceable for shipping. They have not been previously mentioned by navigators, but will now become useful, as during S.E. and E. gales, when the Mulgrave Bar is probably not passable, vessels will have to wait at anchor under High Island, or the Frankland Group.

355. At 9.15 p.m. a large steamer, with long row of brightly-lighted ports, passed south two miles distant to the east of our anchorage.

356. At 5·30 a.m., on the 20th of November, the "Flirt" was under weigh, and standing in to the mouth of the Mulgrave with a fair N.W. breeze, which fell light when close under the land. At 9 a.m. we crossed the bar towed by the whaleboat, carrying six feet over the flats, and at 10 a.m. anchored in the centre of the fine sheet of water at the Junction, in three fathoms, sandy bottom, commanding views up both north and south branches of the river and down the main reach to Point Constantine, over which the Frankland Islands were seen in the offing, N. 73° E.

357. As before stated, the base of Bellenden Kerr is cut off from the river by mangrove swamps, through which a large mangrove creek—named "Harvey's Creek"—runs into the Junction basin 200 yards from the anchorage. One of the principal objects of the Expedition being to accomplish the ascent of Bellenden Kerr mountains, an exploration of this creek and of the north and south branches, to find a landing on sound ground connected with the base of the mountain, was at once commenced.

358. We ascended Harvey's Creek in the afternoon, in a general westerly direction for about two miles direct, although the channel of the creek was extremely tortuous. Here we were able to land upon a small marine plain about half-a-mile broad, covered with coarse reeds and stunted tea-tree; beyond this open ground dense jungles go back half-a-mile to the broad base of the mountain and clothe all its surface. The mountain spurs above us appeared to be extremely rugged, but a more inviting-looking one for ascending came down, apparently, very near a bend of the north branch of the Mulgrave, and I therefore determined at once to examine that arm before attempting the ascent, so that the small quantity of rations which the party would be able to carry should not be thrown away upon struggles to discover a passable route to where their real duties of exploration would actually commence.

359. On Friday, the 21st of November, I started in the whaleboat with Mr. Johnstone, the Botanist, Perry, and crew of eight Native Mounted Police troopers, and ascended the north or main branch of the river for sixteen miles—or a distance direct of about ten miles in a north-west direction from the schooner—towards Walsh's Pyramid and Trinity Harbor.

360. Leaving the schooner, a fine reach, as broad as the Brisbane at the Hamilton but with only four feet at low water, carried us for about a mile and a-half, north by west, close under the south-west spur of Malbon Thompson's Range, which rose from a rocky base of granite, quartzite, and rotten chloritic granite washed by the tide (vide Collection F., Nos. I. and II.), in a steep-hanging dense woodland of rich tropical verdure, to a height of about 900 feet.

361. From this point the range slopes gradually down south-east towards Flirt Point. Beneath its south-west side a large salt-water creek—at the junction of which were neat blacks' gunyahs—comes in from the eastward, isolating a level tract towards the schooner's anchorage, where a tall mass of Kauri pines showed their dark-green heads above the outer fringe of mangroves, and received the name of "Kauri Point," the creek being named Tigbo's Creek.

362. On a bare space on the top of the water-washed rocks above-named were also some picturesque gunyahs of the blacks, and during the whole of our stay the smoke of their camp curled up out of the treetops a hundred yards farther up the hill behind. We saw them daily crossing the river or fishing in their canoes, without molestation.

363. From the hill behind, Malbon Thompson's Range swells into loftier eminences towards the N.N.W. dividing the Vale of Mulgrave from the ocean, the western slopes descending into the valley with a richness of soil and density of woodlands, many thousands of acres of which will doubtless yet contribute to the coffee producing fame of this colony.

364. From the base of this range, under which we had three to five fathoms, the river makes a bold sweep to the west, and, leaving the mangroves behind, runs for two and a-half miles towards the north-west spur of Bellenden Kerr mentioned under clause 358 of this narrative, and which we were desirous to reach.

D

305. At

658

365. At the head of this reach, which approached within one and a half miles of the base of Bellenden Kerr, a sharp bend of the river and E.N.E. reach brought us back towards the base of Malbon Thompson's Range, the breadth of the river contracting to that of the Brisbane at Oxley Creek, with a depth of three fathoms.

366. At eight miles from the Junction the river was fresh at high water, and it thence assumed more the size and appearance of the Brisbane above the Bremer Junction, or of the Lower Herbert, but with deeper water.

367. As we advanced the north spurs of Bellenden Kerr on the left fell away into the low country jungles towards Walsh's Pyramid and Trinity Harbor. On the right the densely-wooded slopes of Malbon Thompson's Range were succeeded by the more lofty Bell's Peaks (mentioned in clause 190 of this narrative), which overlook Trinity Harbor to the N.N.W. and the ocean to the eastward.

368. The course of the river is tortuous, winding from side to side of the level floor of the valley, which is clothed with the thickest jungle, and in the lowest part flooded. In its westerly, and especially its easterly, bends it cuts into the higher lands which slope back, clothed with the same wild and tangled luxuriance of vegetation as that discovered on the Johnstone, to the steeper acclivities of Bellenden Kerr and Malbon Thompson respectively. At fifteen miles up, the banks were twenty feet high, and covered with the same vegetation and with the same rich soil.

369. Sand-banks and snags here prevented our farther ascent, but with a lighter boat I have no doubt we could have reached the base of Walsh's Pyramid, which towered above the end of the terminus reach to the height of 3,016 feet—a bare, steep, and imposing granitic peak, like some storm-beaten "horn" shorn from the summits of the Oberlands and planted on the Australian coast of the Pacific.

370. The Valley of the Mulgrave appeared to come from the westward, between this peak and the northern spur of Bellenden Kerr, on which a smaller peak (Sophia's Peak), of similar shape, showed them to belong to the same upheaval.

371. The sand of the river bed was found to be granite detritus, showing alkalinity. The substratum of Malbon Thompson's Range, cropping out on the east bank of the river bed, thirteen miles up, is quartzite.

372. Numerous neat out-rigger canoes, exactly similar to those seen in Trinity Harbor, eight miles N.N.W. from our highest point reached, also rafts, not seen there, but largely employed for transit on the Johnstone, were seen and examined both going up and returning, but none were taken or in any way interfered with.

373. Numerous round-topped palm-leaf gunyahs occupied picturesque sites on the banks at the bends of the river, generally commanding a view along both reaches. The canoes were all well furnished with fishspears, lines, hand nets, &c.

374. Blacks were seen crossing the reaches ahead of us on our way up, but hid themselves on our approach.

375. Returning down stream in the dark, we passed close to numerous large fires of a blacks' camp, blazing brilliantly on the river bank under the dark forest, giving, with the ruddy reflection in the broad river, the glow and dark shades of the surrounding jungle, combined with the loud yells with which we were hailed from the dense thickets as we passed, a wild and picturesque effect. Visiting the camp, then deserted, a few days later, we found that they had been feasting upon a large crocodile, the debris of which remaining was not pleasant to the olfactories.

376. We returned to the schooner at eight p.m., highly gratified with the valuable discoveries achieved upon a river, our expectations concerning which had certainly been damped by the description in the Coast Sailing Directory, viz., that the boats of H.M.S. "Rattlesnake," after following the course of the river for about two miles, in a westerly direction, found the bed of the river nearly dry.

377. No doubt the large amount of detrition consequent upon the heavy rains and floods of this granitic mountain region has reduced the average depth by sandbanks of considerable breadth and frequency, and it is quite possible that the boats of H.M.S. "Rattlesnake," having ascended to the Junction during a period of uncommon drought and at low water of the lowest spring tides, may have found a large extent of the four-feet banks above our anchorage, nearly if not altogether dry. Under ordinary circumstances, at low water, vessels drawing four feet can ascend from Point Constantine for a distance of ten miles, and at high water for about twelve miles; at that state of the tide vessels drawing seven feet being able to ascend ten miles from the entrance. From the head of navigation flat-bottomed boats will be able to extend communication into a still larger area of this valuable agricultural country.

378. Saturday, the 22nd of November, was occupied by the whaleboat and usual party in searching the lower courses of both branches of the river for fresh water to fill up our tank and casks.

379. Numerous small streams were discovered close to the river, trickling down through the jungles at the bases of Graham's and Malbon Thompson's ranges, but not in sufficient quantity to water the ship; in fact, every evidence exists of the prevalence of an unusual drought this season. The rivers are evidently from one to two feet below their usual volume of fresh water; the small tributaries are only moist, instead of, as indications show that they generally are, channels of briskly running streams, while, equally in the low-lying usually dark jungles, as on the far-up mountain sides, the ferns were dried up and the fine mosses and lichens crumbled between the fingers into powder.

380. Sunday, the 23rd November, was spent quietly on board in the usual manner.

381. On Monday, the 24th, the whaleboat took the "Flirt" in tow, on the flood tide, and proceeded up the north branch, four miles, to "Expedition Bend," nearest the N.E. spur of Bellenden Kerr (vide clause 364 of this narrative). In the afternoon Mr. Johnstone and crew, in the whaleboat, with the dingy in tow, containing two large casks, and all the "breakers," went up to the fresh water and filled them out of the river, returning on board at 4.30 p.m.

382. A thunderstorm from the S.W. passed over and round Bellenden Kerr during the night, accompanied by heavy rain, heralding the near approach of the break of the season, and stimulating us to exertion in getting the ascent of Bellenden Kerr over as soon as possible.

383. Having decided upon despatching Mr. Johnstone and Mr. Hill, with eight troopers, to ascend the mountain on the following morning, every necessary preparation was completed that night. Rations for five days were divided and packed in eight canvas haversacks, which I had made for the purpose, to be carried by the troopers. They also carried some machetes for cutting through the dense jungle,

cantai

canvas water bags to carry a supply of water for camping on the higher spurs and summits of the range, their rifles, and ammunition.

384. I also furnished Mr. Johnstone with a written memorandum of instructions; also with the Government aneroid and one of the thermometers, with which to obtain as many readings as possible, especially at 9 a.m., 3 p.m., and 9 p.m., the hours at which they were always recorded on board.

385. I retained my own aneroid, but it had never been set with the other; I had, however, recorded respective readings of both instruments for some days, and calculated the variations between them as a means of comparing the readings on Mr. Johnstone's return.

386. The morning of Tuesday, the 25th of November, broke clear, fresh, and beautiful. Bellenden Kerr reared his broad massive front, dark-blue and clear cut facing the dawn; only a few fleecy vapors curled up from the deepest glens, and all spoke well for a prosperous exploration, as Messrs. Johnstone and Hill, with eight troopers, thoroughly equipped as described, were landed on the right bank of the river, in high hopes and full of that energy which deserves success, and were at once hid from us—till their return—in the dense jungles.

387. At 3 p.m., having given them sufficient time to return to the schooner—should any unforeseen difficulty of swamps or deep creeks have headed them back from the base of the mountain—I got underweigh and returned to the Junction anchorage, there to watch for their signal smokes as agreed upon, and also to erect a tide gauge, and take soundings of the lower course of the river.

388. From Junction anchorage, we sighted a large topsail schooner, standing S., outside the bar, at 5.30 p.m.

389. During the night, heavy thunderstorms passed over the mountains and swept the Vale of Mulgrave, from S.W., N.W., and S.E. alternately, and we pitied our comrades exposed to its full force on the mountains.

390. At 1 p.m., on Wednesday, 24th, Mr. Johnstone made a smoke signal halfway up the N.E. spur of Bellenden Kerr, which rose like a white slender pillar, and continued for some time. The mountains were clear to-day, and Mr. Johnstone made another signal smoke farther up the same spur at 4.30 p.m. Thunder was heard to the S.W., but it passed N.W., and the night was calm and fine.

391. The morning of Thursday, the 27th of November, was fine, and a smoke was visible near the summit of the N.E. spur of the mountain. The tide gauge this morning, at 4 a.m., showed a rise of only two feet six inches.

392. At 8 a.m., clouds and vapors obscured Bellenden Kerr, sweeping up swiftly from the S.W. and N.W. valleys; at 9 a.m., a light sea breeze lifted them from the centre line of the mountain side. At noon, a fresh north-easter was blowing, and a heavy thunderstorm from the S.W.—the prevalent quarter—obscured the mountain, travelling up against the wind, across the eastern face of Bellenden Kerr. At 2 p.m., a fresh S.E. breeze cleared the clouds off the summit of the mountain, but they settled down again at 3 p.m., and remained so all night; in fact, the mountain was hidden during most part of the day, no signal smokes could be seen, and I was afraid that no view from the summit would be obtained by the shore party.

393. The morning of Friday, the 28th of November, broke fine and clear, and at 10 a.m., a smoke was visible half-way down the N.E. spur, showing that Mr. Johnstone was descending. At 2 p.m., I therefore despatched Perry with two troopers in the whaleboat up the river to Expedition Bend, to bring him back.

394. At 6 p.m., the whaleboat returned on board, bringing Mr. Johnstone and party, all well, after four days' absence, during which he had, against great difficulties, from swamps, and dense bamboo and lawyer scrubs, and rains, succeeded in ascending to the highest peak of Bellenden Kerr, which was reached during the thunderstorm, at noon, the day previous.

395. I leave Mr. Johnstone to tell his story of this interesting expedition, contained in his graphic report, annexed to this narrative. Suffice it here to say, that owing to the geological formation of the range—which proved to be a sharp granitic razor-back, at places only eighteen inches broad along the summit, and so steep that no depth of soil can lodge upon it—the anticipations of botanists concerning it have not been realised, none of the vegetation expected to be found exists upon its slopes, and there is no room for them on the summit.

396. From the broad and massive appearance of Mount Bartle Frere, however, as seen from every point of view, I believe that far greater success would attend an ascent to his more lofty and more ample shoulders.

397. No view was obtained from the summit of Bellenden Kerr, owing to the dark masses of thunder clouds of a storm which was rolling and lightning beneath it; an electrical disturbance, which so depressed the aneroid, that the readings were not at all to be relied on for calculating the height of the mountain. (Vide Appendix B.)

398. From the mountain spurs, however, during the descent, the rich lands of the N. branch of the Mulgrave were seen to encircle Walsh's Pyramid; open grassy plains extending between the base of that mountain and the river.

399. Plains were also seen at the S. end of the S. spurs of Bellenden Kerr, along the low watershed of the Russell and Johnstone rivers; the jungle lands of the former continuing round them into those of the latter, forming one vast sweep of dark-green woodlands, presenting to the eye a repetition of that seen from Basilisk Range at the S. end of this splendid district.

400. Saturday and Sunday, the 29th and 30th of November, were employed in cleaning up fire-arms, filling up with water, &c., writing up journals, and affording a rest to the shore party, after their heavy work and exposure of the last few days.

401. On Monday, the 1st of December, I despatched Mr. Johnstone with whaleboat and full crew of Native Mounted Police, and accompanied by the botanist (Mr. Hill) and Perry, to explore the Russell or S. branch of the river-which I had examined for about eight miles, on the 18th of November.

402. The river was ascended for about fourteen miles towards the plains seen on the Johnstone watershed from the spurs of Bellenden Kerr. The river appears to drain the deep valley between Bellenden Kerr and Mount Bartle Frere, and I feel confident that some of the finest jungle lands in this fertile region will be found in it.

403. The

403. The channel of the Russell is a counterpart of that of the Mulgrave, on a rather smaller scale. Winding from side to side of the lowest level of its valley, nothing can exceed the fertility of the soil of the high banks hollowed out by its waters at the sharp bends into the steep sides of Graham's Range, or the beauty and richness of the lofty overhanging hillsides of jungle, palms, and wild bananas.

404. Five miles up, "Crinum Lily Creek," named from the abundance of those lilies, joined from the N.W., evidently heading in Bellenden Kerr; "Offersia Creek," also draining the slopes of that mountain, enters eight miles up, and was named from the Offersia ferns which adorn its course.

405. I estimate the distance across from the head of boat navigation on the "Russell" to the "Bora Camp" on the Johnstone north branch, at nine to ten miles of elevated ground, all suitable for sugar cultivation, and which, when once opened up, will doubtless be connected by wooden railways, for conveyance of goods, machinery, and produce.

406. At 7·30 a.m., on Tuesday, the 2nd December, we stood down the river with the young ebb tide to the mouth, but were unable to get out—a fresh N.E. breeze blowing straight into the river dead ahead; we therefore anchored in five fathoms inside Point Constantine, and the day was occupied in a thorough examination of both sides of the river for fresh water, in which the party were most successful. Mr. Johnstone found a fine running creek on the south side coming down to the beach out of Graham's Range, about a mile from "Point Constantine." On the north side he also made the valuable discovery of a large lagoon, three-quarters of a mile from "Flirt Point," on the level open forest land, which extends thence to the south end of Malbon Thompson's Range. This lagoon is about 400 yards long and 200 yards wide, and contains an apparently permanent supply of water. On "Point Constantine," Mr. Johnstone found in a large bark gunyah of the blacks, a curious and interesting specimen of defunct humanity, viz., the body of a black gin, doubled up and tied like a roll of spiced beef, and of the same color and somewhat of the same smell. The knees were doubled up to the chin, the heels against the pelvis, the arms doubled close to the sides—the fingers resting on the cheeks, and tied in these positions by split lawyer canes. The body was very much emaciated, and appeared to be stuffed with shreds of mangrove bark, and smoked. When found, it was hanging in the centre of the hut, with a smoke under it. Mr. Johnstone brought it on board, and I have had the pleasure of placing it in the Brisbane Museum. Mr. Johnstone left a couple of blankets and a tomahawk for the bereaved relatives, who would doubtless rightly appreciate the exchange. The head of this mummy is small—the animal organs being developed to distortion, the mental being next to nil; in fact, it is of the very lowest type of human formation.

407. Southward from Point Constantine open forest extends to the base of Graham's Range, suitable for depasturing cattle and horses. From "Flirt Point," northwards, open forest extends between the base of Malbon Thompson's Range and the sea nearly to "Palmer's Point," suitable for a pastoral township commonage.

408. The seaport requirements of this fine **river and** agricultural district will be met by the reservation, on the south side, of "Point Constantine" **and** the land behind it, up to Point Bramston and Graham's Range; and on the north, by the whole **block** of land bounded by the sea to "Flirt Point;" and thence by the river to the sharp westerly bend, one and a-half miles above the Junction anchorage; and thence by a line easterly to the sea; and as a pastoral commonage, the before-mentioned open forest country to "Palmer's Point." (*Vide* proposal reserves on the annexed chart.)

409. These reserves include both water supplies mentioned in clause 406, the only open ground adjacent to navigation, suitable for a town site, fronted by excellent natural wharfage, along the west or inner side of Point Constantine, the south or inner side of "Flirt Point," and in the deep pool of the sharp west bend and the north bank of Tighe's Creek; while along the lower spurs of Malbon Thompson's Range are a great number of beautiful sites of varied altitude, exposure, and scenery of sea and land, suitable for cool suburban homes for future residents, and easy of access.

410. I estimate the available agricultural lands on the Mulgrave and Russell Rivers at between 40,000 and 50,000 acres, which may be looked upon as completing the fertile basin extending from Walter Hill's Ranges on the south to the neighbourhood of Trinity Harbor on the north; bounded all along the west by the lofty coast Cordillera, tapped by five rivers, navigable for light draught vessels, with two excellent harbors—one in its southern, the other in its northern section—for ocean commerce; and the more than probability of discovery of good auriferous country behind it in the interior.

411. In clause 182 of this narrative I stated my belief that the unusual richness of this region is owing to certain coincidences of geological formation, vegetable deposit, and atmospheric currents, and that similar coincidences would produce similar country elsewhere. I believed that I had discovered this repetition in the next great coast basin to the north, between the next most lofty mountains—Arthur Palmer's Range and Thornton's Peaks; and on Wednesday, the 3rd of December, we made sail to northward, to explore it.

412. At 7 a.m., with a light land breeze, and against the flood tide, we stood straight out by the north entrance, direct for the centre of High Island. The peak of Mount Bartle Frere kept over the stern, and carried one fathom, smallest soundings, and that only for a short distance; at three-quarter flood, deepening rapidly to two and a-half fathoms, and dropping suddenly to six fathoms, when we bore away for Fitzroy Island anchorage.

413. The mountains along the whole coast **were hidden in** masses of cloud, and the sultriness of the atmosphere betokened a storm.

414. **In** the afternoon the breeze fell light and baffling, and, with the strong southerly flood setting against us between Fitzroy Island and Cape Grafton, headed us back from our anchorage behind the island.

415. At 9 p.m., heavy thunderstorms were raging all along the coast and mountains, and a black thunder squall was coming up rapidly, but passed to the south and east.

416. At 11 p.m., when between Cape Grafton and Fitzroy Island, the height of the storm came down upon us; a heavy squall, with drenching rain, and thunder and lightning, striking the schooner. Captain Hall, had, however, put three reefs in his mainsail, and taken all headsails in but the inner jib, and she stood up well to it, tearing through the water on an E.N.E. course to clear Fitzroy Island; nothing being visible, even with the aid of the rapid and vivid lightnings, but the rushing sheets of rain, succeeded by the blackest night. Now we were more than ever gratified by the exchange of the cutters for our fine weatherly schooner.

417. At

29

417. At midnight the storm passed away northward along the coast, and out to sea, and we brought up under the N.W. side of Fitzroy Island, 300 yards from the beach, in seven fathoms, sandy bottom.

418. Thursday, the 4th of December, was occupied by the crew and party in washing clothes, filling up with fresh water, &c.

419. A large ketch, with red hull, passed south outside the island at 3 p.m., and Mr. Hill and troopers saw another approaching from the Frankland Islands.

420. Thunderstorms and rain passed far to seaward in the early morning of Friday, the 5th of December; a rain squall passing over Fitzroy Island and the schooner. At 7·30 a.m., we were under-weigh, with a fresh S.E. breeze, for the "Low Islands," off the north end of Trinity Bay, and towards the country of my anticipated discoveries of rich lands on the new rivers seen there.

421. At 2 p.m. the wind fell very light, clouds and rain obscuring the mountains of the mainland. At 5 p.m. Arthur Palmer's Range rose majestically into the clouds to the westward; Island Point bore eight miles N. 265° W., Snapper Island, twelve miles N. 325° N.N.W., Low Islands, six miles N. 335° N.N.W.

422. The night was clear, starlight, and calm, and towards morning a very gentle S.E. breeze carried us to the N.E. of Island Point and into nearer proximity to the river mouth near Mount Beaufort, under Arthur Palmer's Range (vide clause 250 of this narrative), and I watched for dawn to hail the low-lying white river mists under the dark mountain wall of the lofty coast ranges, as evidence of rivers, and rich dank jungles on their banks.

THE RIVERS MOSSMAN AND DAINTREE.

423. Daybreak of the 6th December, found us steering in towards the opening in the land under the loftiest portion of Arthur Palmer's Range, with a light southerly breeze. Island Point stood out towards us into the smooth sea. The Heights of Victory spread their long steep low crest above the coast line—behind them, the fine lofty Harris' Peak rose to the height of 3,578 feet.

424. Passing into the bay to the westward of Island Point, the low land round its southern and western shores to the river opening, which was our destination, appeared to be a network of mangrove creeks. The Heights of Victory rising openly timbered, steep and unbroken to the rear.

425. The anchor was let go on the two fathom line, half-a-mile from the bar of the new river, which I entered in the whaleboat, with Mr. Johnstone, the Botanist, Perry, and crew of Native Mounted Police.

426. We sounded in over the bar with nothing under seven feet at high water, deepening to two fathoms inside. A sand-spit on each side narrows the mouth to about 100 yards—within the entrance, the channel turns abruptly from the S., and shortly again turns from the W.

427. Mangroves extended up either bank for two miles, when the same rich jungles of the Johnstone and Mulgrave took possession of the S. side, on well elevated banks of rich brown loam. In half-a-mile further, dense rich jungles also occupied the N. bank, and appeared to extend over and fill the whole of the large valley beneath, and up the sides of Arthur Palmer's Range, up the slopes of the Heights of Dagmar to the N., and over the lower spurs and acclivities of the southern mountains, without a break.

428. We followed the river up for about four to five miles, when it divided into two branches, one coming from the S., and another from N., evidently draining the broad lofty mountain sides, rising in dark woods and granite cliffs into the clouds, some six miles to the rear—waterfalls of their upper courses precipitating themselves in long white threads from the lofty brows into deep dark jungle-filled valleys below.

429. This river, which was named **the Mossman**, although small, is a very beautiful stream, and suitable for the carriage of produce, **stores**, machinery, &c.—on vessels of light draught of water—to and from the plantations which will in time occupy some of the thousands of acres of rich jungle lands upon its banks.

430. On either side of the mouth of the Mossman, the low coast ranges, the Heights of Dagmar, to the N., and the "Heights of Victory" to the S., sweep back N.W. and S.E., respectively, as at the Mulgrave River, leaving between them and the great mass of Arthur Palmer's Range, a broad valley similar in situation to the Vale of Mulgrave.

431. The vegetation is of the usual lavish variety, beauty, and luxuriance, which characterises the tropical rivers of the North. Cedar appeared to be plentiful, and the jungles were a blaze everywhere with the gorgeous scarlet clusters of numbers of "flame trees," and *Erithrina* (coral tree), in full bloom.

432. I should have liked much to have bestowed more time on a thorough exploration of this river and its surroundings; but the lateness of the season, and the heavy squalls and rains which had already commenced, warned us to quit this part of the coast as soon as possible. We, therefore, returned on board at 11·30 a.m., and stood round the N.W. side of the bay, about a mile off shore, with a moderate E.S.E. breeze, towards the river mouth, which I had seen inside Snapper Island.

433. Several rough coral patches were passed, which are marked in the Admiralty Chart, but appear to be more extensive, and vessels should on no account approach within the five fathom line until opposite the mouth of the Mossman.

434. The Heights of Dagmar descend to the coast in two steep woodland spurs, broken near the beach by sundry lawn-like grassy glades, with pretty scattered oaks (*Casuarina*).

435. From the more northerly spur, the Heights of Dagmar trend away N.W., leaving a broad triangular expanse of low wooded country between them and the Heights of Alexandra on the N ; the beach sweeping round to Cape Kimberley, and only broken two miles inside the Cape, by the broad mouth of the new river, which rapidly opened out to an imposing width.

436. The schooner stood off and on upon the bar, and I proceeded to sound the entrance in the whaleboat, with the usual party, and named this fine river the Daintree, after my friend Mr. R. Daintree, Agent-General of Queensland, the geological formations of the interior explored by him, here coming out upon the coast.

437. The soundings obtained over the bar were six feet (near low water), deepening inside the first reach, which comes from the N., for a mile, to two and three and a-half fathoms.

438. We immediately brought the schooner in with a fine leading breeze, and anchored in the first reach in three fathoms, sandy bottom, well sheltered to seaward by the sand banks, which are dry at low water. The river is about half-a-mile wide, with a sandy beach on each side for some distance in ; the heads being well defined by an isolated clump of tall tea-trees on each—visible for some distance seaward.

439. The

439. The S. head and beach, called "Wyanbeel Point," from the word here used by the blacks for a canoe, is a valuable land mark for steering into the river. It was occupied by a tribe of blacks as we sailed in. They appeared in no way alarmed at our approach, but ran along the beach, gesticulating to us to go away again out of the river. They seemed to get accustomed to our presence, however, before dark, and after great yabbering (chattering) with our Native Mounted Police troopers at the top of their voices, for two hours, without apparently understanding each other, they camped within sight on the beach, close to high-water mark. They had no covering of any description, and lay down in holes in the sand, as is the custom with the inhabitants of Aden, the overlapping points of a few firesticks burning beside them. The inhabitants of Aden have the same custom, and *I have heard* of a gentleman returning from the cantonments to the P. and O. steamer at night, falling headlong into the midst of a family circle, all asleep in one such sandy dormitory.

440. The rain came down with true tropical copiousness nearly all night, but still these naked savages lay in their holes, curled up, without a move; and in the morning of Sunday, the 7th of December, which rose clear and fine, eight of them jumped up, shook themselves, manned a large dug-out outrigger cedar canoe, and came off to the schooner.

441. Although the whole of our party lined the side of the vessel looking at them, they showed no fear; and on receiving a few presents of old shirts, small looking-glasses, &c., they came alongside, when we gave them some blankets, empty bottles, &c., with which they returned on shore, after an hour's palaver, highly delighted.

442. They were met on shore by young and old, male and female, of the tribe, about thirty in number; and their antics, in trying on the shirts—wrong side up—whooping and yelling, laughing and pursuing each other, in their bogle-like attire, were most grotesque and amusing.

443. In a short time the shirts were torn into shreds and bound round their foreheads; and we afterwards found these and the other things left behind in this camp, when they had removed to one more distant.

444. As another evidence of the unchanged manners and customs of these savages during past centuries, Captain Cook describes similar camps, and the same abandonment of clothing,* after the first childish delight of possession, both at Bustard Bay and the Endeavour River.

445. During the afternoon it came on to blow from the south-east; we, therefore, moved the "Flirt" three miles up the river, into a sheltered berth in the second reach—more for protection to the awnings, under which we slept at night, the vessel being in perfect safety.

446. The first reach runs north towards the base of the Heights of Alexandra, and thence turns W.S.W. towards the Heights of Dagmar. Mangroves clothe the banks, broken occasionally by small belts of sound ground clothed with tee-trees and bloodwood.

447. We carried soundings from 2 to 5 fathoms, up both reaches, to our anchorage.

448. From our anchorage the river spread out to about a mile in width, and, at the head of the reach, broke into three branches—that from the W.N.W. being the largest, the south and centre ones large mangrove creeks.

449. A large crocodile showed himself alongside, and was shot by Mr. Johnstone. Very heavy rain fell during the night.

450. On the morning of Monday, the 8th of December, the schooner was moved up the channel—which is here under the south bank, sand banks extending across northwards—carrying 2 to 5 fathoms, and anchored at the confluence of the three branches. Blacks were seen fishing in canoes down the reach.

451. As we came to an anchor the rain clouds, which till then had lain prone over mountains and low country far and near, rose, exhibiting a magnificent panorama of blue, massive, towering distant ranges fronted by the lower densely wooded Heights of Alexandra and Dagmar, which descend towards the river in luxuriant jungles, filling all the broad valley, and giving evidence of many thousands of acres of the same rich agricultural lands which at present make this, and the rivers Johnstone, Mulgrave, Russell, and Mossman, the most beautiful in Queensland—soon to be the gem of Australia.

452. Although, in common with her sister colonies, Queensland possesses deposits of gold, minerals, and gems, enhancing her present prosperity, the production of these may wane; but soils so rich and of so vast extent, opened up by such water carriage, and with such a climate as those alluded to, are a lasting heritage of prosperity in the hands of an industrious and provident people.

453. The north branch, or main stream, appeared to come from the westward, from a gap formed by the convergence and overlapping of these coast ranges, where a gorge between a precipitous hill of the Heights of Alexandra, and a steep cone-shaped hill which formed the western extremity of the Heights of Dagmar, connected with a larger valley above, extending far to the westward, the lofty ranges falling down to the level of its floor, and no physical obstacle being visible between it and the Palmer River diggings, seventy miles to the westward.

454. I started in the whaleboat with Mr. Johnstone, Mr. Hill, Perry, and the usual crew, and examined this branch of the river.

455. About a mile above the schooner, Mr. Johnstone put a snider bullet into the head of another large crocodile; and here the mangroves gave place, on the north bank, to fine jungle, extending back to and up the Alexandra Heights. Here the soundings were reduced by a sandbank to 7 feet.

456. At two and a-half miles above the junction a sharp bend, with 3 fathoms round it, opened a fine reach, running for about a mile and a-half straight to the base of the N.W. terminus hill of the Heights of Dagmar, alluded to in clause 471, above.

457. Both banks of the river were clothed with rich jungles, exactly similar to those on the Johnstone, Mulgrave, and Mossman, and which it may be as well to classify as "Queensland jungle." *It is not scrub*; and to call it so is to mislead as to the luxuriance of a vegetation, which is Indian in its density and massiveness, and as much excels "scrub" in these characteristics as a Calophyllum or Banian does a Briggalow or a Rosewood.

458. At the head of this reach the river makes a bold curve close under the N.W. end of the Heights of Dagmar, and thence sweeps away about N.N.W. between fine jungle-clad banks to the Heights of Alexandra, opposite, and scoops out a sharp escarpment and eight-fathom hole from their base in its sweep round into a beautiful reach from the W.S.W. about a mile long, with certainly the finest river scenery in the colony. 459. The

* "Captain Cook's Voyages," vol. III., pp. 252, 675, and 585.

459. The river valley is here surrounded by a panorama of great beauty; the verdant Heights of Dagmar and Alexandra slope back in more gentle acclivities, undulations, and sheltered valleys—a perfect picture of rich tropical country, fit for almost any description of cultivation. To the W.S.W. the blue mass of Arthur Palmer's Range rose into the clouds beyond the Heights of Dagmar in a long north-west and south-east mountain wall. From the reach, looking back, "Thornton's Peaks" (named after my friend, the Honorable William Thornton, Collector of Customs) towered up to a picturesque crenelated outline of some 4,000 feet close behind the Heights of Alexandra. I venture to say that no river reach in North Australia possesses surroundings combining so much of distant mountain grandeur with local beauty and wealth of soil and vegetation.

460. Messrs. Johnstone and Hill ascended the steep conical hill of the Heights of Dagmar, seen from the mouth of the river, and from its summit of about three hundred and fifty feet elevation had a fine view of the upper valley of the river, which divided about two miles further up, and continued with exactly the same appearance of jungle; one branch for about twenty-five miles to the N.W., the other sweeping southerly round the W. end of the heights of Dagmar for about fifteen miles, draining the large basin between them and Arthur Palmer's Range.

461. The heights on which they stood are composed of slates, tufa, altered Brisbane slates, and some quartz of rather promising appearance, and are openly timbered along their summits, and well grassed upon a strong yellowish brown loam all down their W. and S.W. slopes, presenting much the appearance and quality of the rich lands which I found on the summits of "Sea-view Range" in 1863-64.

462. The value of the discovery of this stretch of excellent grazing country, in the very centre of the rich jungle agricultural lands of the Daintree and Mossman rivers, speaks for itself; for, in the absence of such grazing accommodation, future settlers would be dependent upon the growth of artificial grasses and tubers on expensively cleared woodlands, for the support of stock, for ration and farming purposes.

463. From the proximity of Hann's track out of "Weary Bay," through an open forest pastoral country, about fifteen miles to the N.W., I believe that the agricultural lands on the north bank of the river are also well supplied with available grazing country to the rear.

464. The position of a high wooded range to the W.N.W., at the head of the river valley, also coincides with the "high scrubby range" of his chart, and I am strongly of opinion that the river heads which he followed up into his western slopes, and supposed to be those of "Bloomfield's Rivulet," are really the heads of the Daintree, which thus overlap those of the Palmer.

465. At the head of the reach we had six feet of water, which was nearly fresh, with a fine sandy bottom ; and from the appearance of the river, the continuance of the tideway higher up, and the length, breadth, and low level of the floor of its valleys, we came to the conclusion that an agricultural region lay before us, which would require a fortnight's additional time and finer weather to thoroughly explore.

466. The season had now completely broken; deluges of rain, squalls, and violent thunderstorms were of daily occurrence, and the hurricane season, so dangerous upon this coast, had begun. The health of the party suffered from the muggy heat and usual miasmatic influences of mangrove inlets, and new country subjected to alternations of heavy rains and steaming hot sunshine, and I was necessitated to come to the conclusion that on this occasion we could not hope to complete the exploration of this beautiful and valuable region ; we had, however, discovered its existence, and formed a good general idea of its qualifications, and I sincerely trust that the Government will do me the honor to send me back after the rainy and hurricane season, to finish its exploration, and fill in the valuable details of this and much more fine country, doubtless existing between Cape Bedford and Cape York.

467. I therefore felt it to be my duty to return to more settled weather to the south, and to report to Government the discovery of this previously unknown river and agricultural district, the existence of which was never even suspected.

468. It was with much regret that we turned the boat's head down stream ; but a more enjoyable feast of beautiful scenery I have never previously experienced in Queensland, enhanced by feelings of gratitude that to us was permitted the privilege of first making known to our fellow-colonists the existence of this valuable and hitherto unknown region also. There are but few excitements so thorough in their enjoyment as those of the explorer when he finds himself suddenly a discoverer, and unravels gradually warp and woof of beauty and utility of the intricacies of his discoveries.

469. Mr. Hill obtained some very interesting specimens of palms, and samples of soils.

470. A very heavy easterly squall, with drenching rain, met us in the teeth en route down stream, and we arrived on board, drenched, at 6.30 p.m.

471. During our stay up the river we every day saw some of our aboriginal friends fishing in their canoes in the big reach, but they never again came near us until we returned to the mouth of the river, when Messrs. Johnson and Hill fraternised with and restored confidence to them again.

472. On Tuesday, the 9th December, I sounded the south branch, which turned out to be a man-grove creek with three fathoms of water, and some open ground, which would do for building purposes, on its west bank, half-a-mile from the junction ; and in the afternoon the schooner beat down the river, to our old anchorage in the first reach, against an easterly breeze.

473. At sundown a ship under sail was seen off the low islands.

474. On the morning of the 10th December I despatched Mr. Johnstone, accompanied by Mr. Hill, and detachment of Native Mounted Police, to examine the lands up to Cape Kimberley on the north and around Wyanbeel Point on the south side of the river, and report upon their capabilities for township sites ; and proceeded myself to make a rough survey of the bar, which I completed by noon.

475. Mr. Johnstone returned on board and reported good building ground all the way to Cape Kimberley, along the top of the beach, facing the sea, but narrow ; around Wyanbeel Point there is also a considerable area extending along the beach towards the heights of Dagmar. There is also fresh water in swamps and native wells.

476. I should recommend reserves to be made on both sides of the river, but the north side presents this advantage—that along the slopes of Cape Kimberley and the Heights of Alexandra, only a mile from the township, the future inhabitants will have a vast number of fine airy and beautiful sites for suburban residences, so necessary and desirable in this tropical climate.

477. There is a fine extent of natural wharfage along the N. bank of the river, and although backed

by

32

by mangroves, the land is well elevated and of sufficient soundness to allow conversion by an artificial surfacing of road metal from Cape Kimberley, and sand from the beach, to reclaim a township site of any required extent. For the nucleus of the town, and for all the first business requirements of a young settlement, there is room on the shore lands behind Hall's Point, and thence to Cape Kimberley.

478. At 1.30 p.m. we got under weigh and stood out to sea, carrying nothing under nine feet soundings on the bar an hour past high water, and stood away S.E. for Fitzroy Island with a moderate N.E. breeze and fine weather. At 6 p.m. the Low Islands lay four miles N.E. on our port beam. A large topsail schooner, which showed no colors in answer to ours, appeared to be at anchor under the W. side of the reef; the breeze fell very light at midnight; Harris' Peak bearing N.W., and Double Island eight miles S.S.E.; an easterly current setting us in fast towards the land.

479. At 11 a.m. on Thursday, the 11th of December, we anchored close in to the watering place on Fitzroy Island, whence we filled up the water casks and tank. At noon we again got under weigh and stood away for the Frankland Islands with fresh N.W. breeze; heavy thunderstorms over Bellenden Kerr and the coast.

480. At 2.30 p.m. we passed the N.E. headland of High Island, and hove to to endeavor to fix the position of the rock, but being high water could see nothing of it. When about a mile to the S.E. of it, however, the break over it was plainly discernible.

481. At 3.30 p.m. we anchored under the W. side of No. 1 Frankland (Coconut Island), in thirteen fathoms, muddy bottom; landed and shot forty Torres Straits pigeons as a change of diet for all hands.

482. At daybreak on the 12th of December, a cutter was sighted between us and the land, standing S.E. At 6.30 a.m. we were under weigh and standing in towards Cooper Point, as, having left the last weather behind us, I determined to return to the Johnstone River to take some more observations and soundings, and to come to a final determination as to the reserves for public purposes which it would be necessary to recommend.

483. At 3 p.m. we anchored in the first reach of the Johnstone, inside Coquette Point, in three fathoms. The afternoon was cloudy and sultry with very light breeze from the N.E.; the thermometer at 3 p.m. being 95°, the aneroid standing at 29.72.

484. At 7 a.m. on Saturday, the 13th of December, by Mr. Hill's desire, I despatched him, with Mr. Johnstone and the usual crew, in the whaleboat, up the river, to penetrate further into the jungles and to obtain more samples of soils, &c.

485. At 11 a.m. some blacks showed on Coquette Point; they were painted white all over, excepting from the waist to below the knees, to represent shipwrecked seamen with their trousers rolled up, and shouted to us, rather cleverly imitating the tones of whitemen's voices, and made many signals to us to go ashore, but no notice was taken of them whatever.

486. The boat party returned on board at 6 p.m., having been successful in penetrating the jungles on the N. bank. They also made the wonderful discovery of a fig-tree 150 feet 9 inches in circumference 3 feet from the ground.

487. I regretted being unable to see this magnificent tree, but, without desiring to detract in any way from the value of the discovery, I must say that I do not anticipate that a sectional cut from the tree would show an unbroken solid slab of fifty feet in diameter, but, rather, that like the one of the same description in the East Indies, the section would show the joinings of hundreds of twisting stems, layer above layer, which first strangled out a tree round which they had formed a network, and thereafter continued to enfold each other during many years till the exterior presented the appearance of a solid stem, the interior section more that of mosaic work.

488. Service was held on deck at 11 a.m. on Sunday, the 14th of December, during which the same blacks, similarly disguised, came out on Coquette Point, and after putting up a tent pole, left from our old camp, to represent a mast, imitated hauling on ropes to get a sail up. They then pretended to kill one of their number on the beach, in evident allusion to the way in which the unfortunates of the "Maria's" raft were disposed of, waving their arms towards the outer sea beach, and shouting "whitefellow."

489. I sent Mr. Johnstone ashore after service with a detachment of his troopers, to search for any traces of white men, but none were to be found.

490. He found, however, that they had disinterred the remains of a poor murdered "Maria's" man close by, and to that they probably wished to draw our attention in bravado. We were the more confirmed in this opinion from the facts, not only that before Mr. Johnstone landed—mistaking our inaction for fear—they began shouting and yelling, and dancing their war corroboree, and making use of the most insulting gestures towards us, but that he found an armed mob of them lying hidden in the jungle behind Coquette Point, ready to attack any one who might be deceived into going ashore by their signals.

491. This treacherous system of decoying or inviting people by signals to land, is probably as old as the earliest discoverers of Australia, the first on whose credulity they could have practised it. Captain Cook alludes to it in his voyages, vol. III., page 409, in Botany Bay, and commends the "great prudence" of his officer, Mr. Gore, on whom it was tried, for declining the invitation.

492. I have seen it on many different parts of the N.E. coast, and known many cases where a rash disregard of that prudence which the great navigator commended, has cost many a poor fellow his life. I have had myself to bury the stripped and mutilated remains of wholly unoffending victims—one, a gentleman who had dined with me on the previous day, who I warned of the treachery of the aborigines along the coast; and who answered, "Well, I never did the blacks any harm, and I don't think they will touch me." Next day he was dead on an island beach, with twenty-four spear wounds in his neck and shoulders, and gashed from head to feet, to the bone, with knives.

493. Very serious is the responsibility which those safe dwellers in cities take to themselves who preach in the public prints "peace where there is no peace," but too frequently "sudden destruction;"—who, by systematic declaration, against all evidence, of the perfect normal innocence and harmlessness of these savage cannibals, lull the inexperienced into a sentimental pity for them—a reckless disregard of their personal safety from aboriginal outrage that has caused more bloodshed in this colony than has resulted from all the outrages committed against them put together; which, while placing the lives of our countrymen in danger, at the same time encourages the aborigines to more and more daring outrages which, in turn, can only be stayed by a still more copious effusion of blood, which is abhorrent to civilized people. 494. Monday,

494. Monday, the 15th of December, was devoted to washing and cleaning arms, &c., &c. All hands, except the defence force on board, being sent ashore to the watering place creek for that purpose. In the evening, heavy rain and squalls of rain and wind came in from seaward (S.S.E.), and at 11 p.m. it was blowing a gale.

495. The gale moderated towards morning of Tuesday, the 16th of December, which broke fine with moderate E.N.E. breeze.

496. With Mr. Johnstone I went up the river in the whaleboat to the Junction (Nind's Camp), accompanied by Mr. Hill and Perry, with crew of native police. I took another line of soundings right up, and cross-bearings to fix all bends and reaches of the river, and we examined its shores, especially from Coquette Point to Nind's Creek, for natural wharfage and fresh water. A large extent of the former extends round the proposed reserve on Coquette Point side from opposite Crocodile Rock to Nind's Creek. Of the latter, two small trickling rills were found, which, in ordinary seasons, are likely to produce a considerable supply.

497. At noon and during the afternoon and night we had a recurrence of heavy rain squalls from the sea, and at 2 a.m. of the 17th it was blowing hard with squalls of rain and hail; clearing up at dawn, when a light land breeze came down the rivers, the clouds gradually lifting off the ample sides of Mount Bartle Frere.

498. At 7 a.m. we stood out of the Johnstone against the flood tide, and at three-quarters rise carried seven feet and nine feet over the bar. A heavy swell was rolling in from seaward, but at this time of tide there was no break across the channel.

499. At 8 a.m. we stood away for Mourilyan Harbor, but rain and squalls came up from the S.E., and the breeze becoming variable, heading us off on every tack, we did not reach the heads till daylight on Thursday, the 18th of December, when we stood in and anchored opposite Camp Point; closed with the N. head, about three hundred yards from shore, in two and a-half fathoms, sandy bottom.

500. At 8·15 a.m. I accompanied Mr. Johnstone and Mr. Hill in the whaleboat, with Perry and crew, to explore Walter's Creek and Armit's Creek, on the opposite side of the harbor. We ascended the former for about three miles of a tortuous course, but with bold water throughout, except at the mouth, where it is reduced to about three feet at low water by the sandbanks.

501. On the west bank of the creek, near the head of navigation, a long narrow ridge of sandy loam, covered with forest and scrubby under-growth, connects this tributary of Mourilyan Harbor with the wide areas of rich jungle lands extending west to the South Johnstone and north to the main branch of the river at the junction of Nind's Creek, the head of boat navigation, on which certainly could not be farther than two miles over flat marine plains.

502. We then ascended and sounded Armit's Creek, on the south side of Ethel Hill, but after a tortuous course of about four miles, it broke up into small branches without reaching the jungle lands. From only one point on the main creek would it be possible to carry a tramway over a rather more elevated and open part of the mangrove swamps, where a few scrub bushes appeared, to the jungle lands. At some future and not distant day this may be required, thus affording three channels of water carriage from these agricultural lands to Mourilyan Harbor, viz., by the Moresby and Armit's and Walter's creeks.

503. At 5 p.m. Mr. Hill was landed on the north shore, under Hilda Hill, to plant cocoanuts, coffee, &c., &c.

504. On Friday, 19th December, a party was sent ashore to water the ship from a fine new spring, found a hundred yards east of Camp Point, running over the rocks to the beach. At 7.30 a.m. Mr. Hill was landed at Camp Point, with Native Mounted Police Corporal Sam and three troopers, to collect botanical specimens on Georgie Hill.

505. At 9 a.m. I accompanied Mr. Johnstone and troopers, and Mr. Tighe, and Mr. Hall, the master of the "Flirt," in the whaleboat, and landed at Esmeralda Hill, which we ascended, and from its open summit I again took compass bearings to now well known objects on the Johnstone River valley, and made sketches of the harbor.

506. At 2 p.m. I went out through the harbor entrance in the dingy with the master of the "Flirt," and fixed the positions of Perry's and Hall's Rocks—the first referred to in clause 47 of this narrative, the latter discovered by Mr. Hall, of the "Flirt," in a very dangerous position off the entrance. It stands a dark sharp rock about four feet above low water off the S. head; No. III. Barnard Island, on with outer Hayter Point Rock bearing N. 143° S.E.; Camp Point on with N. end of Ethel Hill N. 257° W. To avoid this rock, vessels entering the port must open out Camp Point well from the south-shore. In going about from the starboard to the port tack the morning before, the schooner must have gone right round the rock then covered at high water. I would strongly recommend a thorough marine survey of the harbor and entrance to be made without delay, previous to settlement and consequent arrival of shipping.

507. At 7 a.m. on Saturday, the 20th of December, we got under weigh, and stood into the harbor entrance with a moderate and fair land breeze; but such was the strength of the flood tide rushing in against us that we did not succeed in passing out to sea till slack water, at 10 a.m., when the N.E. sea breeze supplanting the land one, we had to tow out with the whaleboat.

508. At noon, we were off the North Barnard Islands, and sighted the lofty peaks of Hinchinbrook, and the Rockingham Ranges far away to the southward. The smoke of a steamer was seen approaching from the direction of Cape Sandwich.

509. When standing in to the anchorage under No. II. South Barnard Island, the steamer was seen about four miles off heading outside of us, and I despatched Mr. Johnstone in the whaleboat to intercept her, and ask if she carried a mail for the expedition.

510. As Mr. Johnstone lay in waiting in her route, I was surprised to see her sheer off E., and go right round the boat a quarter of a mile from it, and resume her course, until sighting us, now at anchor under the island, with the blue ensign flying, she ran right in and anchored close to us, Mr. Johnstone following with a fresh fair wind in his lug sails.

511. She proved to be the small paddle steamer "Annie," from Adelaide, via Tasmania and Australian Ports, bound for Port Darwin; and that, seeing Mr. Johnstone and a crew of blacks endeavoring to cut him off, the captain and crew believed them to be wild aboriginals with hostile intent, when they evaded them, and ran in for protection to the blue ensign as described. They had their arms ready loaded on deck to give Mr. Johnstone a warm reception.

E

512. In the afternoon a shore party was landed to get wood and water; two hours' capital shooting was obtained, nearly one hundred Torres Straits pigeons being shot by Mr. Johnstone, myself, and two others.

513. Heavy thunderstorms, as usual, raged along the coast and mountains.

514. At 4 a.m. on Sunday, the 21st of December, we got under weigh and stood south for Dunk Island. The breeze fell light at 8 a.m., when the steamer "Annie" passed us, bound for Cardwell to repair machinery.

515. At noon, we passed the "Annie" at anchor off the sand spit of Dunk Island, and stood round Tam o' Shanter Point into Kennedy Bay, for the purpose of exploring the north branch of Commodore Burnett's river "Hull," off the embouchure of which we anchored at 1 p.m., in two and a-half fathoms sandy bottom.

516. At two p.m., I started in the whaleboat with Mr. Johnstone and Mr. Hill, with Perry and eight troopers, and ran into the mouth of the river under the lug sail before a spanking breeze, lowered it at the bar, and sounded in.

517. The mouth of the river is immediately under the S. face of a hill forming the S.W. end of Kennedy Bay, and is about three hundred yards broad, but choked with sandbanks, shoaling the water at low tide to three feet.

518. About a mile in, the river comes from the N.W., N.N.W., and then N. and N.N.E., with an average depth of six feet, deepening three miles up to two fathoms, and then shoaling again to the former soundings.

519. The general N. and S. course of the river for about six miles here is parallel to the coast between Tam o' Shanter and Cooper's Points; its banks are clothed with rich jungles and soils—samples of which were obtained—running through to the coast in valleys of dense vegetation, suitable for agriculture. (*Vide* clause 31 of this narrative.)

520. About nine miles from the mouth, the river turned from the W.N.W. towards the base of Hunchback Mountain, all the lower slopes of which and the neighbouring lower hills are clothed with dense woodlands and jungles.

521. We were in hopes of reaching these jungles beyond the mangrove belt which extended along the W. side of the river; but in three miles, boat navigation was difficult, and from a high tree no break in the mangroves could be seen by the native mounted troopers for some miles.

522. From this point, the summit of Hunchback bore N. 263° W., and thence we returned on board through heavy thunder and lightning and a deluge of rain, arriving alongside at 8.30 p.m.

523. A heavy easterly swell rocked us to sleep on this the last night of our pleasant cruise in the "Flirt," and the clouds rained down their last passion upon us from a dark leaden sky, but the early morning came in fair and bright starlight.

524. At 2·40 a.m. we got under weigh, and stood along the coast for Port Hinchinbrook with a light N.W. breeze, and at 11 a.m. the "Flirt" ran alongside the Cardwell Jetty, and made fast, thus bringing to an end one of the most important and prosperous expeditions which have ever successfully explored the Australian coast—an expedition marred by no serious accidents to detract from its unvaried good fortune, and productive of results of the most valuable description to the colony at large.

525. It was with much gratification that we received the hearty congratulations of, and warm welcome from our good friends in Cardwell, many well-known faces meeting us on the jetty.

526. On Tuesday, the 23rd, the surplus stores and all specimens and curios, &c., &c., were landed from the schooner, and she was paid off; but before bidding her farewell, I must take this opportunity of publicly thanking Mr. Tighe, the owner, and Mr. Hall, the master of the "Flirt," for the unvarying zeal, precision, and carefulness with which they navigated the vessel and performed every duty required of them connected with the Expedition, and for the courtesy which they invariably showed to our whole party.

527. The stores and arms, &c., were transferred to the Native Mounted Police and Gold Escort, according to instructions telegraphed to me by the Commissioner of Police.

528. By telegraphic order of the Colonial Secretary, of date the 24th December, 1873, I proceeded to Brisbane by the first steamer, s.s. "Boomerang," deposited the specimens of rocks, soils, and curios with Mr. Staiger, in the Queensland Museum, Brisbane, and reported myself to the Honorable Arthur Macalister, who had succeeded the Honorable A. H. Palmer as Colonial Secretary and Premier of Queensland.

529. It affords me much pleasure to express my high appreciation of the services of my second in command, Inspector Robert Johnstone, and the valuable assistance and cheerful co-operation which I received from him on all occasions. The zeal and efficiency of the fine body of Native Mounted Police under his charge also was worthy of all praise, and reflected the greatest credit upon their officer. I have also much pleasure in endorsing Mr. Johnstone's remarks as to the energy and judgment evinced by John Perry, in charge of the police boat, his skill as a boatman, and his discipline and diligence as a seaman.

GENERAL REMARKS.

Doubtless the results of this expedition, and of that of Mr. Hann in the interior which preceded it, will bear fruit in the settlement of the Cook district with a rapidity hitherto unequalled since the first blush of gold discoveries in Australia.

Already, in the short space of four months, Cooktown and the Palmer River diggings have acquired a population of some three thousand souls, and some sixty vessels are said to be about to be "laid on" for the Endeavour from the Australasian ports at the termination of the rainy season. And so soon as the agricultural lands on the new rivers have been thrown open by Government, the occupation of the soil will be, if a little less, still sufficiently rapid and probably more permanent.

The influx of so large a population—the sudden occupation of so large a district, in addition to the present wealth and population of the Kennedy District—gives a new importance to Northern Queensland in the eyes of neighbouring countries, and has already brought the requirements of its development under the active consideration of the Government.

Already it is traversed by the telegraph line, which, touching its principal seaports, will soon be joined to the Anglo-Indian system at the present terminus at "Norman Mouth."

Already

35

Already coasting steamships call at all its ports, and the Royal Mail Steamers *via* Torres Straits bring them into immediate communication with the great centres of Indo-European commerce.

Before the discovery of the Palmer diggings its gold fields were very extensive, and their yield of most important dimensions, while the successful production of sugar in the Port Mackay and Lower Herbert districts has attracted much and deserved attention.

To foster the development of these rich gold fields—to stimulate the cultivation of these new and magnificent lands, is the privilege of the Government which I serve—to assist it by every information in my power, gained during fifteen years' connection with the North as explorer, settler, Government officer, and Parliamentary representative, is my earnest wish.

The elements, at present retarding approach to the new Northern Eldorado, cannot long restrain the onslaught of some three thousand energetic men upon its hidden wealth.

It is fortunate that by the provisions of the Land Bill of 1868 the whole of the valuable agricultural coast country just discovered is free from vested interests injurious to its rapid development, and is now open to public selection.

The development of that country will in a short time add probably six new seaports to the coast of this colony, yielding most important additions to the customs' revenue; while the inducements which it holds out to immigration from Great Britain and the Australian Colonies will rapidly enhance the importance and influence of Queensland, either individually or as a member of a federal group.

For the general advantage of the whole colony, and advancement of these districts, the formation of a railway from Port Denison to the Gulf of Carpentaria is hardly premature.

Passing through the Ravenswood, Charters Towers, Gilbert Ranges, and Etheridge gold fields, the traffic of large auriferous districts would be secured, and forming a direct trunk line from the Pacific to the Gulf, Indo-European passengers and mails would have a means of rapid and safe transit, meeting the mail steamers at either terminus to convey them to their respective destinations.

Doubtless more northerly ports are ambitious of the distinction of being the Pacific terminus, but I speak advisedly in recommending Port Denison.

Its harbor is safe and land-locked, and has excellent facilities for landing and shipping. From its position, by shortening as much as possible the steam service on the Pacific side, it presents more decided advantages to the southern portions of this and the whole of the other colonies; while, from the configuration of the country, a railway could traverse the proposed route, ascending and descending the central table land of 2,000 feet elevation without crossing a single difficult range—an advantage possessed by no other seaport of the Kennedy District.

Ultimately, the certain future junction of the intercolonial railways, and extension of those of Southern Queensland, *via* Springsure and Clermont, to Ravenswood, will bring the whole Australian traffic through these districts, whose many valuable mineral lodes, now unremunerative from length of carriage, will contribute to the revenue of the railway and the wealth of the colony.

Much discussion has lately taken place as to the most advisable route for telegraphic communication with the Endeavour and the Palmer diggings. By laying a submarine cable along the coast, from Cardwell to Mourilyan Harbor and the mouths of the Johnstone, Mulgrave, Daintree, and Endeavour rivers, and then overland to the Palmer, the requirements of these districts would be met at the least possible annual outlay, combined with perfect safety to the line from the blacks. A shore line would necessarily traverse some sixty miles of dense jungles and some of the most broken country in Queensland, and would at all times be subject to interruption from falling timber, rapid under-growth, and the aborigines, who infest the whole coast country in large numbers—a daring and hostile race.

From Tam O'Shanter Point to Cape Tribulation, with the exception of the granitic coast ranges from Bell's Peaks to Island Point, schistose rocks prevail, with quartz and conglomerates; the slates similar to those on the Gilbert Ranges, the back country having a very auriferous appearance. Mr. Hann gives a glowing account of the auriferous appearances up the Mitchell and Palmer Rivers. Towards the back of the Great Bartle Frere, Bellenden Kerr, and Arthur Palmer coast ranges, the granites gave place to slates and quartz-reefs; the gold in the latter river, which has since increased in quantity and weight as the prospectors have ascended it, appearing to have come from the upper parts of its course. I should therefore infer that there still exists a wide extent of auriferous country in the valleys of this mountain region to repay the prospectors for the toils and hardships of exploring this still unknown country. Should it be found to extend to the back of Bellenden Kerr Ranges, probably Trinity Harbor may be required, adding a seventh to this line of new seaports—its central position on the coast line opposite the Great Trinity opening through the Barrier reefs, placing it in a favorable position for the ocean trade of the district.

From our observations in the Valley of the Daintree, I believe that a road may be found from the head of navigation into the auriferous back country in a N.W. direction, past the N. end of the high ranges, which there sink to the general level of the country. Doubtless some jungle would have to be cut through, but from its position relative to Mr. Hann's track over open country between those ranges and Weary Bay, it cannot be extensive and no high range has to be crossed.

Lately the Daintree has been ascended in the steamer "Annie" by two officers and a detachment of Native Police, to endeavor to find this route, but have reported it impracticable, and thence proceeded to Weary Bay, whence from Bloomfield Rivulet they report sanguine expectations as to discovery of a passable dray route.

From the description given, I am still of opinion that a route may be found out of the Daintree Valley, as it is evident to me that the party sent by the Commissioner of Police, with the laudable object of bringing assistance to the starving miners at the Palmer, had not taken the route which I recommended to him, viz., N.W., so as to strike Hann's track at that end of the high ranges.

From Admiral King's and other descriptions of the Bloomfield Rivulet by nautical authorities, I do not anticipate the discovery of a suitable port in its estuary; while from Mr. Hann's description of the precipitous mountains which surround it, over which he had much difficulty in extracting his party, although travelling with packhorses only, I do not expect the discovery of a passable dray road thence in the desired direction.

If

36

If a thorough exploration of the Daintree outlet fails to supply the required route, I do not doubt that Mr. A. C. Macmillan or Mr. Sub-inspector Douglas will succeed in opening communication from Cooktown to the south-west of the present track. Personally speaking, I have no doubt whatever as to the existence of the former, and firmly believe that Mr. Hann or my late second in command, Mr. Inspector Johnstone, would trace it out without difficulty, if I was permitted personally to communicate my ideas on the subject to them. Mr. Hann crossed the route which I propose only eight or ten miles from head of navigation on the Daintree, and, from the mountain above his sixty-fourth camp (*vide* Hann's report, page 11, and camp 64 on chart) he had a bird's-eye view of the entire district which I propose to cross. Mr. A. C. MacMillan would very soon convert the route into a good practicable dray-road of some eighty-five miles in length. It is only to be regretted that it has not yet been thoroughly examined, as, doubtless, the six to eight hundred stalwart miners cooped up by the floods in enforced idleness at Cooktown would have much preferred sweeping down with axe and "cross-cut" a broad track through the Daintree jungles to the open country and thence cutting down creek crossings and sidings with pick and shovel to the desired Eldorado, leaving their communications open behind them to the coast, and heading every river.

The settlement of this new district will stimulate the valuable pearl-shell, bêche-de-mer, and turtle fisheries along this coast, and afford facilities for bringing the protection of these industries under the control of legislative enactment.

The immediate throwing open to selection of the agricultural lands along this coast will complete the successful launching of this magnificent district upon a brilliant future, to be developed by the strong arms and indomitable energies that have, in less than a century, made Australia what it is.

But one more district remains to be explored and settled, viz., to the head of the York Peninsula, and then we are face to face with new Guinea and the Malayan Archipelago. The coast rim of settlement of Australia may then be said to have received the keystone to its structure of colonisation, and —granted the acquisition of Fiji accomplished—the formal Imperial annexation and settlement of New Guinea will then alone remain to complete the consolidation of British power and commerce in the Pacific and Indian Oceans, and to secure to these Australasian Dominions a self-contained power, which shall be their strength in whatsoever international complications may sweep the face of Europe and Asia.

During fifteen years my humble services have been much given to exploring the interior in part, and the sea-coast *in toto*, from Broad Sound to Cape Bedford, and to the opening up of the adjacent districts by settlement. I again place my services at the disposal of the Government for the purpose of completing that last link of exploration from Princess Charlotte's Bay to Cape York, and trust that I may be permitted to do so during the favorable season of the year which is about to commence.

When the above enterprises have been realised, the Queensland settlement in Torres Straits will assume a position of very considerable international importance on one of the principal ocean gateways of the world.

G. ELPHINSTONE DALRYMPLE.

F.R.G.S., P.M., G.C.

APPENDIX A.

LIST OF MINERAL SPECIMENS COLLECTED BY THE EXPEDITION, 1873.

Expedition No.	Museum No.	Locality.	Description.
		MOURILYAN HARBOR.	
A 1	8	Base of Hilda Hill	Ferruginous slate.
2	4	Ethel Hill	Rotten mica slate.
3	10	Esmeralda Hill	Quartz.
4	5, 6	Ditto	Mica and quartz (Greisen).
5	9	Hilda Hill	Ferruginous chloritic mica slate.
6	3	Camp Point	Talcose rock.
7	1	Hilda Hill	Chloritic mica slate.
8	2	Ditto	ditto.
9	7	George Hill	Quartz, with manganese and iron ore.
10	12	Ethel Hill	Quartz.
		GLADY'S INLET AND NORTH AND SOUTH BRANCHES OF THE RIVER JOHNSTONE.	
B 1	72	Perry's Point	Chloritic slate.
2	82	Ditto ...	Rotten chloritic mica slate.
3	79	Ditto ...	Chloritic mica slate.
4	75	South Branch	Yellow ochre.
5	80	Nind's Junction Camp ...	Quartz, with a little mica.
6	81	Near ditto, South Branch	Micaceous slate.
7	76	Ditto	Talcous schist.
8	74	Rocky Point, South Branch ...	Ferruginous conglomerate.
9	77	South Branch	Volcanic tufa.
10	70	Ditto	Slate.
11	73	Ditto	Sandy ochre.
12	83	Basilisk Range ...	Quartz.
13	71	Ditto ...	Fine grained sandstone.
14	78	South Branch	Ferruginous sandstone.

37

APPENDIX A—*continued.*

LIST OF MINERAL SPECIMENS COLLECTED BY THE EXPEDITION, 1873—*continued.*

Expedition No.	Museum No.	Locality.	Description.
		GLADY'S INLET AND NORTH AND SOUTH BRANCHES OF THE RIVER JOHNSTONE—*continued.*	
D 1	66A	Bora Camp	Diorite.
2	66	Head of Boat Navigation	Quartz.
3	67	Ditto	Fine-grained rotten granite.
4	65	Ditto	Slaty quartzite.
5 }	69 {	Ditto	Quartz.
6 }		Ditto	(Bag of wash-dirt) auriferous drift.
7	68	Near Bora Camp	Diorite.
		NORTH-EAST COAST AND ISLANDS.	
E 1	21	No. 1, Frankland Islands	Quartz, mica, and hornblende.
2	21A	Ditto	Diorite.
3	13	Fitzroy Island	Decomposed hornblende granite.
4	24	Double Island	White stratified sandstone.
5	23	Macalister's Range	Quartz.
6	14	Double Island	Slate allied to the Brisbane slate.
7	22	Ditto	Quartz.
		ENDEAVOUR RIVER.	
8	18	Endeavour River	Granite.
9	19	Endeavour River (6 miles up)	Ferruginous sandstone.
10	16	Endeavour River (Macmillan's Look-out)	Slate allied to the Brisbane slate.
11	17	Endeavour River	Quartz.
12	26	Endeavour River (present township site)	Chloritic slate.
13	25	Endeavour River (present township site)	Chloritic granite.
14	15	Endeavour River (present township site)	Burnt decomposed slate.
15	29	Annan River	Rotten sandstone.
16	31	High Island	Quartz, hornblende-mica.
17	28	Ditto	Tourmaline.
18	27	Ditto	Rotten granite.
19	38	Ditto	Quartz with mica.
20	35	Mossman River	Granite drift (sand from river bed).
21	32	Cape Kimberley	Quartz with chloritic slate.
22	34	Ditto	Slate allied to the Brisbane slates.
23	37	Ditto	Altered slate.
24		Ditto	Ditto.
25	30	Ditto	Quartz with chloritic slate.
26	28A	Ditto	Slate allied to Brisbane slates.
27	60	Moresby Range	Chloritic slate.
28	58	Ditto	Ferruginous conglomerate.
29	64	Ditto	Chloritic slate.
30	59	Glady's Inlet	Chloritic mica slate.
31	63	Ditto	Quartz.
32	61, 62	Ditto	Quartz.
33	36	Fitzroy Island	Quartz.
34	20	Ditto	Decomposed granite (sort of red Kaolin Bolus)
		RIVERS MULGRAVE AND RUSSELL.	
F 1	47	Malbon Thompson's Range	Rotten chloritic granite.
2	54, 55	Ditto	Rotten granite.
3	51	Ditto	Quartzite.
4	50	Bed of river	(Sand) granitic detritus.
5	52	Russell River	Granite.
6	49	Bellenden-Kerr Mountain	Rotten gneiss.
7	48	Ditto	Quartz.
8	(55)	Ditto	Ditto.
9	56	Ditto	River sand sheins.
10	46	Graham's Range	Kind of gneiss.
11	45	Ditto, Point Bramston	Gneiss.
12	53	Ditto	Granite.
		RIVER DAINTREE.	
G 1	41	Heights of Dagmar	Slate allied to Brisbane slate.
2	43	Ditto	Tufa, decomposed trachyte.
3	39	Ditto	Altered (Brisbane) slates.
4	40	Ditto	Quartz.
5	42	River bed	Sand.
6	44	Ditto	Gneiss.

G. ELPHINSTONE DALRYMPLE.

APPENDIX B.

670

38

APPENDIX B

METEOROLOGICAL OBSERVATIONS BY THE NORTH-EAST COAST EXPEDITION, 1873.

Date.	Hour.	Locality.	Wind.	Barometer.	Thermometer.	Remarks.
					Degrees.	
1873.						
Sept. 22	9 a.m.	Gould Island Camp	W.	30.15	75	Light, hazy over the land.
"	3 p.m.	Ditto	S.E.	30·7	80	Fresh, fine ; smokes over the coast.
"	9 p.m.	Ditto	Calm	30·15	74	Calm, sultry ; cloudy from S.E.
" 23	9 a.m.	Ditto	S.E.	30·10	78	Strong, thick over sea and land.
"	3 p.m.	Ditto	S.E.	30·10	78	Ditto.
"	9 p.m.	Ditto	S.E.	30·5	75	Gale, with heavy rain.
" 24	9 a.m.	Ditto	S.E.	30·	68	Heavy gale, rain-squalls.
"	3 p.m.	Ditto	S.E.	30·15	75	Heavy gale, rain-squalls, very thick over the land.
"	9 p.m.	Ditto	S.E.	30·20	72	Ditto.
" 25	9 a.m.	Ditto	S.E.	29·15	75	Gale, very thick over the land.
"	3 p.m.	Ditto	S.E.	30·10	70	Ditto.
"	9 p.m.	Ditto	S.E.	30·10	75	Ditto.
" 26	9 a.m.	Ditto	S.E.	No readings : recording officer absent in consequence of sea-swell.		Ditto.
"	3 p.m.	Ditto	S.E.			Ditto.
"	9 p.m.	Ditto	S.E.			Ditto.
" 27	9 a.m.	Ditto	S.E.	30·10	74	Strong wind, clearing.
"	3 p.m.	Ditto	S.E.	30·15	78	Strong, fine.
"	9 p.m.	Ditto	S.E.	30·10	75	Ditto.
" 28	9 a.m.	Ditto	S.E.	30·10	75	
"	3 p.m.	Ditto	S.E.	30·10	75	Gale, thick over the land.
"	9 p.m.	Ditto	E.	30·10	74	Gale, thick over the land, driving scud.
" 29	9 a.m.	Ditto	S.E.	30·20	74	Moderate, fine.
"	3 p.m.	Anchor.—Dunk Island	E.	30·5	77	Ditto.
"	9 p.m.	Ditto	E.	30·12	69	Light breeze, fine.
" 30	9 a.m.	Ditto	S.	30·15	78	Light breeze, very fine.
"	3 p.m.	Off S. Barnard Islands	E.S.E.	30·3	76	Ditto.
"	9 p.m.	Anchor.—No. 3 N. Barnard	S.S.W.	30·10	73	Ditto.
Oct. 1	9 a.m.	Off Double Point	S.W.	30·12	73	Ditto.
"	3 p.m.	Anchor.—Mourilyan Harbor	E.N.E.	30·2	77	Fresh breeze, fine.
"	9 p.m.	Ditto	E.	30·10	73	Ditto.
" 2	9 a.m.	Ditto	E.N.E.	30·12	76	Calm, fine, light outside harbor.
"	3 p.m.	Ditto	S.E.	30·10	78	Light breeze, fine.
"	9 p.m.	Ditto	W.	30·10	74	Ditto.
" 3	9 a.m.	Ditto	E.S.E.	30·12	76	Light breeze, fine, hot.
"	3 p.m.	Ditto	S.E.	30·3	79	Ditto.
"	9 p.m.	Ditto		30·5	73	Calm, fine.
" 4	9 a.m.	Ditto	S.W.	30·10	77	Light breeze, fine.
"	3 p.m.	Glady's Inlet	E.S.E.	30·	77	Fresh breeze, fine.
"	9 p.m.	Mouth Johnstone River	W.	30·10	67	Light breeze, fine, cool.
" 5	9 a.m.	Ditto	W.	30·10	74	Light breeze, fine, cool, cloudy.
"	3 p.m.	Ditto	E.	30·3	79	Fresh breeze, cloudy over the mountains.
"	9 p.m.	Ditto	W.	30·10	74	Light breeze, fine, clearing off mountains.
" 6	9 a.m.	Anchor.—Nind's Camp, Johnstone River		30·10	77	Calm, cloudy, sultry.
"	3 p.m.	Ditto	N.E.	30·5	78	Light breeze, showers.
"	9 p.m.	Ditto		30·10	75	Calm, cloudy, like rain.
" 7	9 a.m.	Ditto		30·5	79	Calm, fine.
"	3 p.m.	Ditto	E.N.E.	30·	80	Fresh breeze, fine.
"	9 p.m.	Ditto		30·	78	Calm, fine.
" 8	9 a.m.	Ditto	E.N.E.	30·10	77	Light breeze, very fine.
"	3 p.m.	Ditto	E.S.E.	30·3	81	Fresh breeze, fine.
"	9 p.m.	Ditto		30·5	76	Calm, fine.
" 9	9 a.m.	Ditto	S.E.	30·15	78	Light breeze, cloudy.
"	3 p.m.	Ditto	N.N.E.	30·10	77	Ditto.
"	9 p.m.	Ditto	W.	30·15	73	Very light breeze, fine.
" 10	9 a.m.	Ditto	S.E.	30·12	74	Ditto.
"	3 p.m.	Anchor.—Bora Camp, Johnstone River	S.S.E.	30·10	78	Fresh breeze, fine.
"	9 p.m.	Ditto	W.	30·20	72	Light breeze, fine.
" 11	9 a.m.	Ditto	S.E.	30·20	76	Fresh breeze, fine.
"	3 p.m.	Ditto	S.E.	30·10	78	Ditto.
"	9 p.m.	Ditto	W.	30·18	73	Light breeze, fine.
" 12	9 a.m.	Ditto	S.E.	30·15	76	Fresh breeze, fine.
"	3 p.m.	Ditto	S.E.	30·10	78	Ditto.
"	9 p.m.	Ditto	W.	30·20	73	Light breeze, fine.
" 13	9 a.m.	Ditto	N.N.W.	30·10	78	Fresh breeze, fine.
"	3 p.m.	Ditto	N.E.	30·5	78	Ditto.
"	9 p.m.	Anchor.—Mouth Johnstone River	W.	30·5	76	Light breeze, hazy to seaward.
" 14	9 a.m.	Off Cooper Point	S.	30·10	75	Light breeze, fine.
"	3 p.m.	Anchor.—No. 1 Frankland Island	N.E.	30·3	81	Fresh breeze, fine.
"	9 p.m.	Ditto	S.E.	30·10	76	Fresh breeze, cloudy on the land.
" 15	9 a.m.	Anchor.—Fitzroy Island	E.	30·18	76	Fresh breeze, cloudy.
"	3 p.m.	Anchor.—Rocky Island	E.	30·10	81	Ditto.
"	9 p.m.	Ditto	S.E.	30·12	76	Ditto.

39

APPENDIX B—*continued.*

METEOROLOGICAL OBSERVATIONS BY THE NORTH-EAST COAST EXPEDITION, 1873—*continued.*

Date.	Hour.	Locality.	Wind.	Barometer.	Thermometer.	Remarks.
					Degrees.	
1873.						
Oct. 16	9 a.m.	Anchor.—Rocky Island	S.E.	30·17	81	Moderate breeze, fine.
"	3 p.m.	Entrance to Trinity Harbor	S.E.	30·29	75	Ditto.
"	9 p.m.	Anchor.—Trinity Harbor	S.E.	30·29	74	Heavy rain-squalls.
" 17	9 a.m.	Ditto	S.E.	30·10	78	Strong breeze, cloudy.
"	3 p.m.	Ditto	S.E.	30·5	78	Ditto.
"	9 p.m.	Ditto	W.S.W.	30·10	74	Light breeze, fine.
" 18	9 a.m.	Ditto	S.S.E.	30·10	75	Light breeze, cloudy.
"	3 p.m.	Anchor.—Double Island	S.E.	30·5	78	Fresh breeze, squally.
"	9 p.m.	Ditto	E.S.E.	30·8	75	Moderate breeze, fine.
" 19	9 a.m.	Ditto	S.E.	30·10	75	Squally.
"	3 p.m.	Ditto	S.E.	30·10	75	Strong breeze, fine.
"	9 p.m.	Ditto	2.E.	30·	75	Moderate breeze, fine.
" 20	9 a.m.	Ditto	S.E.	30·5	79	Fresh breeze, fine.
"	3 p.m.	Ditto	E.S.E.	30·	83	Ditto.
"	9 p.m.	Ditto	S.	30·10	75	Light breeze, fine.
" 21	9 a.m.	Ditto	S.E.	30·10	75	Moderate breeze, fine.
"	3 p.m.	Ditto	S.E.	30·	81	Fresh breeze, fine.
"	9 p.m.	Ditto	E.S.E.	30·10	78	Light breeze.
" 22	9 a.m.	Ditto	S.	30·10	74	Moderate breeze, fine.
"	3 p.m.	Ditto	S.E.	30·	80	Fresh breeze, fine.
"	9 p.m.	Ditto	S.E.	30·10	76	Moderate breeze, fine.
" 23	9 a.m.	Off Red Cliffs	S.	30·10	75	Fresh breeze, fine.
"	3 p.m.	Anchor.—Snapper Island	E.S.E.	30·	82	Ditto.
"	9 p.m.	Ditto	E.S.E.	30·8	76	Ditto.
" 24	9 a.m.	Off Cape Tribulation	S.	30·8	78	Fresh breeze, fine.
"	3 p.m.	Off Walker Point	S.E.	30·2	78	Strong breeze, fine.
"	9 p.m.	Anchor.—Endeavour River	S.E.	30·8	78	Strong breeze, fine ; driving scud ; gale outside.
" 25	9 a.m.	Ditto	S.E.	30·	78	Strong breeze, fine.
"	3 p.m.	Ditto	S.E.	30·	78	Fresh breeze, fine.
"	9 p.m.	Ditto	S.E.	30·5	78	Ditto.
" 26	9 a.m.	Ditto	S.E.	30·5	78	Ditto.
"	3 p.m.	Ditto	S.E.	29·95	80	Ditto.
"	9 p.m.	Ditto	S.E.	30·5	78	Ditto.
" 27	9 a.m.	Ditto	S.E.	30·	85	Moderate breeze, fine.
"	3 p.m.	Ditto	S.E.	29·95	85	Ditto.
"	9 p.m.	Ditto		29·95	82	Calm, fine.
" 28	9 a.m.	Ditto	E.N.E.	30·	78	Moderate breeze, fine.
"	3 p.m.	Ditto	E.	29·95	84	Ditto.
"	9 p.m.	Ditto		30·	80	Calm, fine.
" 29	9 a.m.	Ditto	E.S.E.	30·	80	Moderate breeze fine.
"	3 p.m.	Ditto	S.E.	30·5	84	Fresh breeze, fine.
"	9 p.m.	Ditto	S.E.	30·5	83	Moderate breeze, fine ; flying scud.
" 30	9 a.m.	Ditto	S.E.	30·5	84	Ditto.
"	3 p.m.	Ditto	S.E.	30·	83	Ditto.
"	9 p.m.	Ditto	S.E.	30·5	82	Ditto.
" 31	9 a.m.	Anchor.—"Three Isles"	E.S.E.	30·10	83	Ditto.
"	3 p.m.	Ditto	S.E.	30·	86	Ditto.
"	9 p.m.	Ditto	S.E.	30·8	82	Light breeze, fine.
Nov. 1	9 a.m.	Off Endeavour River	S.E.	30·10	83	Ditto.
"	3 p.m.	Off Double Island	S.E.	29·95	87	Ditto.
"	9 p.m.	Anchor.—High Island		30·	87	Calm, fine.
" 2	9 a.m.	Off Mourilyan Harbor	S.E.	30·5	82	Light breeze, fine.
"	3 p.m.	Anchor.—Cardwell	E.S.E.	30·	87	Ditto.
"	9 p.m.	Ditto		30·5	84	Calm, fine.
" 14	9 a.m.	Ditto	N.N.W.	30·5	78	Light breeze, fine ; smokes over the land.
"	3 p.m.	Anchor.—Dunk Island	N.E.	30·	86	Fresh breeze, fine ; smokes over the land.
"	9 p.m.	Ditto	W.	30·5	84	Light breeze, fine.
" 15	9 a.m.	Ditto	N.E.	30·5	82	Very light air, sultry ; smokes over land and sea.
"	3 p.m.	Ditto	N.N.E.	30·5	88	Fresh breeze, sultry ; smokes over land and sea.
"	9 p.m.	Ditto	W.	30·10	84	Light breeze, sultry ; smokes over land and sea.
" 16	9 a.m.	Ditto	W.	30·10	78	Light breeze, fine.
"	3 p.m.	Ditto	E.	30·	83	Moderate breeze, fine.
"	9 p.m.	Ditto	W.	30·10	80	Light breeze, fine.
" 17	9 a.m.	Off Clump Point	S.E.	30·12	80	Light breeze, fine ; clouds and smoke over the land.
"	3 p.m.	Off Johnstone River	E.S.E.	30·5	80	Moderate breeze, fine, clear.
"	9 p.m.	Anchor.—No. 2 Frankland Island	E.	30·10	83	Light breeze, fine, clear.
" 18	9 a.m.	Off the bar, Mulgrave River	S.	30·10	83	Moderate breeze, fine.
"	3 p.m.	Off High Island	S.E.	30·	88	Ditto.
"	9 p.m.	Anchor.—No. 2 Frankland Island	S.E.	29·97	84	Moderate breeze, fine ; heavy clouds to N.

40

APPENDIX B—*continued.*

METEOROLOGICAL OBSERVATIONS BY THE NORTH-EAST COAST EXPEDITION, 1873—*continued.*

Date.	Hour.	Locality.	Wind.	Barometer.	Thermometer.	Remarks.
1873.					Degrees.	
Nov. 19	9 a.m.	Off High Island	...	30·5	83	Calm, fine.
,,	3 p.m.	Ditto	...	30·	90	Calm, fine, hot.
,,	9 p.m.	Anchor.—Off High Island	E.	29·95	86	Light breeze, fine.
,, 20	9 a.m.	Crossing the bar of the River Mulgrave	S.E.	30·5	83	Ditto.
,,	3 p.m.	Anchor.—Junction of Rivers Mulgrave and Russell	E.N.E.	29·95	84	Ditto.
,,	9 p.m.	Ditto	W.N.W.	29·95	86	Ditto.
,, 21	9 a.m.	Ditto	S.W.	30·10	77	Moderate breeze, fine.
,,	3 p.m.	Ditto	N.E.	30·5	84	Fresh breeze, fine.
,,	9 p.m.	Ditto	E.N.E.	30·5	82	Light breeze, fine.
,, 22	9 a.m.	Ditto	S.E.	30·10	78	Moderate breeze, fine.
,,	3 p.m.	Ditto	S.E.	30·	87	Fresh breeze, fine.
,,	9 p.m.	Ditto	S.W.	30·5	83	Light breeze, fine.
,, 23	9 a.m.	Ditto	S.E.	30·2	80	Moderate breeze, fine.
,,	3 p.m.	Ditto	S.E.	29·95	84	Ditto.
,,	9 p.m.	Ditto	W.	29·97	82	Light breeze, fine.
,, 24	9 a.m.	Ditto	N.	29·95	79	Ditto.
,,	3 p.m.	Anchor.—Expedition Bend, Mulgrave River	N.	29·80	86	Fresh breeze, fine.
,,	9 p.m.	Ditto	S.E.	29·92	84	Very light air, fair, cloudy; thunderstorm at 8 p.m. to seaward.
,, 25	9 a.m.	Ditto	S.E.	29·64	83	Very light air, sultry.
,,	3 p.m.	Anchor.—Junction of Rivers Mulgrave and Russell	S.E.	29·53	87	Cloudy, thunderstorms round Bellenden-Kerr Mountains.
,,	9 p.m.	Ditto	S.	29·60	85	Heavy rain-squalls; heavy thunderstorms all round.
,, 26	9 a.m.	Ditto	N.E.	29·64	81	Fresh breeze, fine, clear over mountains.
,,	3 p.m.	Ditto	E.N.E.	29·52	84	Fresh breeze, fine, thunder to S.W.
,,	9 p.m.	Ditto	N.W.	29·63	83	Light breeze, fine, cloudy over mountains.
,, 27	9 a.m.	Ditto	E.N.E.	29·87	82	Light breeze, fine, misty over mountains.
,,	3 p.m.	Ditto	S.E.	29·82	84	Fresh breeze, cloudy over Bellenden-Kerr Mountains.
On board schooner	9 p.m.	Ditto	S.W.	29·83	82	Fair, cloudy.
By Mr. Johnstone, ascending Bellenden-Kerr Mountains	6 a.m.	Second shoulder, N.E. spur Bellenden-Kerr Mountains	S.W.	26·30	68	Misty, very light breeze, fair.
,,	Noon	Highest Peak	E.	24·33	64	Thunderstorms passing below summit.
,,	9 p.m.	Camp at North Summit	S.W.	25·78	68	Moderate breeze, rain.
Nov. 28	9 a.m.	Anchor.—Junction of Rivers Mulgrave and Russell	N.W.	29·90	82	Fine, clear, light breeze.
,,	3 p.m.	Ditto	S.W.	29·55	85	Rain, light breeze.
,,	9 p.m.	Ditto	N.W.	29·60	84	Fine, moderate breeze, clear.
,, 29	9 a.m.	Ditto	N.W.	29·69	80	Light breeze, fine, clear.
,,	3 p.m.	Ditto	N.E.	29·60	84	Fresh breeze, fine; mountains clear.
,,	9 p.m.	Ditto	N.W.	29·55	83	Very light air, fine; mountains clear.
,, 30	9 a.m.	Ditto	N.E.	29·69	84	Ditto.
,,	3 p.m.	Ditto	N.E.	29·75	85	Thunderstorms to the W.; mountains obscured.
,,	9 p.m.	Ditto	N.W.	29·80	85	Very light breeze, fine, clear.
Dec. 1	9 a.m.	Ditto	S.E.	29·86	83	Light breeze, fine, cloudy.
,,	3 p.m.	Ditto	N.E.	29·86	85	Moderate breeze, fine.
,,	9 p.m.	Ditto	S.W.	29·87	84	Very light breeze, cloudy.
,, 2	9 a.m.	Anchor.—Point Constantine	N.E.	29·93	83	Fresh breeze, fine; cloudy on mountains.
,,	3 p.m.	Ditto	N.E.	29·75	85	Ditto.
,,	9 p.m.	Ditto	N.E.	29·82	84	Light breeze, fine.
,, 3	9 a.m.	Off bar of River Mulgrave	N.N.E.	29·88	84	Light breeze, fine, cloudy.
,,	3 p.m.	Off Grey Peaks	N.N.E.	29·72	91	Fresh breeze, fine.
,,	9 p.m.	Off Fitzroy Island	S.	29·80	81	Heavy thunderstorms all along the land and out to sea, S. and S.E., which struck the schooner at 11 p.m.
,, 4	9 a.m.	Anchor.—Fitzroy Island	N.N.E.	29·82	82	Fresh sea breeze, fine, clear.
,,	3 p.m.	Ditto	N.	29·72	84	Moderate breeze, fine.
,,	9 p.m.	Ditto	N.	29·77	84	Light breeze, fine, cloudy.
,, 5	9 a.m.	Off Cape Grafton	E.	29·86	83	Fresh breeze, cloudy.
,,	3 p.m.	Island Point, N. 270° W. 10 miles	E.S.E.	29·77	89	Light breeze, cloudy.
,,	9 p.m.	Off Island Point	S.	29·80	86	Ditto.
,, 6	9 a.m.	Off bar of River Mossman	S.W.	29·82	86	Light breeze, fine; mountains obscured.
,,	3 p.m.	Off bar of River Daintree	E.S.E.	29·82	90	Moderate breeze, cloudy, hot.
,,	9 p.m.	Anchor.—Inside River Daintree	...	29·89	88	Calm, fine; heavy rain at midnight.
,, 7	9 a.m.	Ditto	E.S.E.	29·95	84	Light breeze, cloudy; 10 a.m., heavy rain.
,,	3 p.m.	Ditto	S.E.	29·90	81	Fresh breeze, squally.
,,	9 p.m.	Ditto	S.E.	29·92	82	Very light breeze, fine, cloudy.

41

APPENDIX B—*continued.*

METEOROLOGICAL OBSERVATIONS BY THE NORTH-EAST COAST EXPEDITION, 1873—*continued.*

Date.	Hour.	Locality.	Wind.	Barometer.	Thermometer.	Remarks.
1873.					Degrees.	
Dec. 8	9 a.m.	Anchor—Inside River Daintree	W. ...	29·95	80	Very light breeze, fine, cloudy.
„	3 p.m.	Ditto	S.E. ...	29·85	84	Fresh breeze, fine.
„	9 p.m.	Ditto	S.W. ...	29·92	83	Light breeze, steady rain.
„ 9	9 a.m.	Ditto	S. ...	29·96	81	Light breeze, cloudy.
„	3 p.m.	Ditto	S.E. ...	29·87	85	Moderate breeze, fine.
„	9 p.m.	Ditto	S.E. ...	29·90	84	Strong breeze, fine.
„ 10	9 a.m.	Ditto	S.E. ...	29·97	82	Light breeze, fine.
„	3 p.m.	Off bar of River Daintree ...	N.E. ...	29·89	85	Moderate breeze, fine.
„	9 p.m.	Off Mount Garioch ...	N.N.E.	29·89	85	Light breeze, fine.
„ 11	9 a.m.	Off Macalister Range	N.W. ...	29·89	84	Moderate breeze, fine.
„	3 p.m.	Off High Island ...	N. ...	29·78	92	Moderate breeze, thunderstorms **over** Bellenden-Kerr Mountains.
„	9 p.m.	Anchor.—No. 1 Frankland Island	N.N.W.	29·82	78	**Fresh** breeze, fine, cloudy.
„ 12	9 a.m.	Off Point Cooper ...	S.S.E.	29·84	88	Light breeze, fine.
„	3 p.m.	Anchor.—Inside Coquette Point, Johnstone River	N.E. ...	29·72	93	Light breeze, cloudy.
„	9 p.m.	Ditto	W. ...	29·78	87	Light breeze, cloudy, **sultry**.
„ 13	9 a.m.	Ditto	...	29·85	87	Calm, sultry.
„	3 p.m.	Ditto	N.N.E.	29·80	94	Fresh breeze, fair, cloudy.
„	9 p.m.	Ditto	N.E. ...	29·85	88	Light breeze, fine.
„ 14	9 a.m.	Ditto	N.E. ...	29·95	83	Ditto.
„	3 p.m.	Ditto	N.E. ...	29·91	86	Ditto.
„	9 p.m.	Ditto	...	29·95	87	Calm, sultry.
„ 15	9 a.m.	Ditto	E. ...	30·3	83	Strong, fair, cloudy over mountains.
„	3 p.m.	Ditto	S.E. ...	29·97	83	Squally, rain showers.
„	9 p.m.	Ditto	S.S.E.	30·2	85	Heavy rain-squalls, and blowing strong with heavy rain-squalls all night.
„ 16	9 a.m.	Ditto	E.S.E.	30·5	83	Moderate breeze, fair, cloudy.
„	3 p.m.	Ditto	E.N.E.	29·97	85	Moderate breeze, squally ; rain.
„	9 p.m.	Ditto	S.E. ...	30·	84	Heavy rain-squalls all night.
„ 17	9 a.m.	Off the bar, Johnstone River	S. ...	30·5	82	Squalls, with thick weather to S.E. ; rain.
„	3 p.m.	Off Moresby Range ...	S.E. ...	30·	85	Strong breeze, fine.
„	9 p.m.	Ditto	S.E. ...	30·	83	Light breeze, fine.
„ 18	9 a.m.	Anchor.—Mourilyan Harbor	E. ...	29·97	84	Light breeze, fair, cloudy.
„	3 p.m.	Ditto	E.N.E.	29·88	85	Light breeze, fine.
„	9 p.m.	Ditto	W. ...	29·90	84	Calm, fine.
„ 19	9 a.m.	Ditto	W. ...	29·95	80	Light breeze, fine.
„	3 p.m.	Ditto	E. ...	29·83	83	Moderate breeze, fine ; hot.
„	9 p.m.	Ditto	N.W. ...	29·80	84	Light breeze, fine.
„ 20	9 a.m.	Off Mourilyan Harbor	W.S.W.	29·90	81	Ditto.
„	3 p.m.	Anchor.—No. 2 South Barnard Island	N.N.E.	29·80	93	Moderate breeze, fine.
„	9 p.m.	Ditto	N.E. ...	29·85	87	Light breeze, fine ; thunderstorms along the land passing N.
„ 21	9 a.m.	Off Clump Point	N. ...	29·67	87	Light breeze, fine, hot.
„	3 p.m.	Anchor.—Kennedy Bay	N.N.E.	29·77	90	Light breeze, sultry ; thunderstorms along ranges.
„	9 p.m.	Ditto	W. ...	29·85	83	Light breeze, heavy rain.
„ 22	9 a.m.	Off Murray River ...	N.W. ...	29·87	82	Light breeze, fine.
„	3 p.m.	Port Hinchinbroke ...	N.E. ...	29·89	88	Ditto.
„	9 p.m.	Ditto	...	29·90	83	Calm, fine.

G. ELPHINSTONE DALRYMPLE.

42

Police Camp, Lower Herbert,
30th December, 1873.

SIR,

I have the honor to forward you the following Report of the Expedition.

September 9th.—Left police camp for Cardwell to join Expedition.
September 10th.—Unpacking stores, &c.
September 11th.—Ditto   ditto.
September 12th.—Ditto   ditto.
September 13th.—Ditto   ditto.
September 14th.—Ditto   ditto.
September 15th.—Ditto   ditto.
September 16th.—Returned to police camp for Trooper Sam.
September 17th.—Started for Cardwell taking Trooper Sam.
September 18th.—Waiting arrival of cutter " Coquette."
September 19th.—Ditto   ditto.
September 20th.—Formed camp on Gould Island.
September 21st.—Full dress parade, service at 11 a.m.
September 22nd.—Went to Cardwell in police boat and returned at 1 a.m. same night.
September 23rd.—Mr. Dalrymple and Mr. Tompson went to Cardwell in police boat.
September 24th.—In camp on Gould Island.
September 25th.—Cutter " Coquette " arrived in Cardwell; I went to Cardwell in police boat.
September 26th.—Returned to Gould Island in " Coquette," with Sub-Inspector Tompson.
September 27th.—Stowing stores in cutters.
September 28th.—Full dress parade, service at 11 a.m., taking ballast in " Flying Fish" in the afternoon.

September 29th.—The Expedition made a final start; the members consisting of G. Elphinstone Dalrymple, Esquire, leader; Sub-Inspector Tompson, 2nd; Sub-Inspector Johnstone, in charge of Native Police; Walter Hill, Esquire, Botanist; Dodd S. Clark, in charge of cutter "Coquette," with crew of two men; Captain Hall, of the "Flying Fish," with crew of two men; police boat in charge of John Perry, police boatman; John Vickers, orderly to leader; Charles Maidman, cook to the expedition; and thirteen Native Troopers. We sailed at 10·30 a.m., all hands well, and a fair wind; we reached Dunk Island at 2 p.m., when I went on shore to pitch the camp, on a brigalow ridge on the N.W. point of the island, close to the watering place, the cutters anchoring about half-a-mile off us, and the boats drawn up on the beach, Mr. Nind and party camping near us; this was my tenth visit to this very interesting island. I was over the island with my gun but only saw some scrub hen (Megapodius tumuli), a small swift, and two kinds of flycatcher; but some of the creeks were ornamented with most beautiful fern trees of two kinds, and a very great variety of handsome ferns and orchids in full bloom. Three of the troopers missed me and were absent all night.

September 30th.—Sailed from Dunk Island, at 10 a.m., and anchored off the No. III. North Barnard at 5 p.m., when I landed to form camp, and, by permission of our leader, I went over it, taking my gun, and shot some scrub hen and Torres Strait pigeon.

October 1st.—I went off again at daylight and succeeded in shooting my first specimen of the glorious Victoria riflebird. The shading of the colors baffles my power of description; the female bird is of a very sober brown color, their food consists of insects and fruits, and I saw them sucking honey from flowers; their movements are very like the woodpecker's, their note is very like the bower bird. I also shot a brown dove and black butcher bird. I saw also a new bird, it was black with rather short tail, with two long white feathers out of the centre of the tail, the bird was about the size of a quail, I think it belonged to the kingfisher tribe. The Barnard Islands are five in number and on the South Barnard and No. III. North, water can be obtained in small quantities; they are all covered with jungle, and in the season are visited by turtle and Torres Strait pigeon in immense numbers. We sailed at 7 a.m., for Mourilyan Harbor, and arrived there at 12 noon, and camped on the south side under a most beautiful spreading fig-tree, close to two streams of good running water; the point is called Camp Point in the chart. This was my fourth visit here, and bore evidence of being a favorite camp of the blacks, as on every visit I found several gunyahs freshly built, and as we entered the harbor we saw six canoes making up the Moresby River, which empties into the harbor, as fast as they could. I saw specimens of the rifle-bird here, and shot Torres Strait pigeon, a new kind of fruit eater about the size of a satin bird but marked like a guinea fowl.

October 2nd.—We explored the Moresby and went up about a mile beyond my farthest on my former visit. On the south side we found a large pandanus and tea-tree swamp; but on the north side we found some patches of good scrub land which I had mentioned in my former report; the soil here is very good and of a red color. Mr. Nind ascended the river in his boat and succeeded in finding a most beautiful new dendrobium in full bloom. We returned to camp at 10 p.m., and found everything all right. Captain Hall kept all hands well supplied with fish, which he caught with a mesh net.

October 3rd.—Started at 8 a.m. in the police boat to ascend Esmeralda Hill, a beautiful little green hill on the south side of the harbor; we found a blacks' camp at the base, and from the summit we had a most magnificent view of the surrounding country, of the harbor and the Moresby River; it was estimated that the whole of the hills were suitable for cultivation.

October 4th.—We left Mourilyan Harbor in the police boat, leaving Sub-Inspector Tompson and Mr. Hill to come with the cutters, and entered the river discovered and reported by me on my former visit, and, though dead low water, we went straight in the boat and found three feet of water in the shallowest place on the bar; but we did not look for the channel, and when the tide made we stood straight in with the cutters and anchored off the point on the south side, inside the river. We saw blacks on both sides of the river. I went out with the troopers in the afternoon, and in my absence two canoes passed above the camp. At sundown the blacks came down and took the fires away we had made for dinner on the opposite side. We pitched our camp on "Coquette" Point, on the south side, and kept watch all night, but nothing occurred.

October

October 5th.—By orders of our leader, I went up the river in the police boat, to find suitable place for pitching camp and for the cutters to lay, and about six miles up, at the junction of the south branch with the main stream, I found a good camp on the point which was called Nind's Camp, as he camped there that night ; there were sixteen feet of water at dead low water here. I saw two rafts with blacks on board, and moved them off our camping ground ; also one who was prowling round, taking stock of us. We returned to camp at 5 p.m.

October 6th.—Mr. Dalrymple took the cutters up to the new camp at Nind's Camp, and I was congratulated by all the members of the party in having discovered the river, and our leader honored me by naming it after me. Mr. Hill and Mr. Nind told me it was a finer river than the Brisbane, at the junction of the two branches ; they both expressed themselves astonished and delighted at the appearance of the river, soil, and most luxuriant vegetation on its banks, which are high and a long way above any flood marks : the soil is superior to any they had seen for agricultural purposes. After breakfast we went up the South Johnstone for twelve miles, and found it to be a river larger than the Herbert, and no flood-marks near the top of the banks anywhere ; the soil all equally good and rising from the river backwards, thereby causing the whole of the drainage to flow into the river. The timber consisted of cedar, one specimen of which measured twenty-three feet nine inches in circumference, three feet from the ground ; Moreton Bay chesnut, quandong, whitewood, Cardwellia, Eugenia, and several other large trees that were new to me ; also fan palm and Alexandra palm. There are some rapids, with rocky bottom, about eight miles up. We returned to camp at sundown.

October 7th.—We again ascended the south branch and went up about fourteen miles, and then landed on the east side and cut a track through the jungle to a small range about two miles off, which was named "Basilisk Range," after H.M.S. "Basilisk," which we ascended and got a splendid view of Mourilyan Harbor and the Moresby River, the North and South Johnstone, with the Bellenden Kerr Ranges in the distance. The extent of good available sugar land is almost inexhaustible, and of the very richest ; in evidence of which I may mention the native ginger, a plant which on the Herbert and other southern rivers grows about four feet high, here reaches twenty-five feet, and you walk under it like walking through a palm grove ; and the wild banana grows immense sizes and height—same were measured five feet nine inches in circumference and growing to a height of thirty-five feet. We returned to camp at 9 p.m.

October 8th.—Mr. Dalrymple stayed in camp. Sub-Inspector Tompson and myself went up to the large cedar tree and ran a line back for some distance to see what the back country was like, and found it to rise and the soil all equally good. We came to a small creek at the back, in a depression, draining into the river. I shot a most beautiful honeysucker, like a humming bird—rich brown back, rifle-green throat, and bright canary-colored breast ; legs and eyes black. I also shot pigmy goose, black duck, two kinds of kingfisher, a cuckoo, and a green-winged dove. We also explored a creek running to the N.W., about half-a-mile from Nind's Camp, on the west side of the south branch. We here saw immense quantities of bamboo, and the creek was called " Bamboo Creek." I believe this is the first river where the bamboo has been found indigenous. I shot the scrub turkey, or "Tallagalla," here.

October 9th.—Mr. Dalrymple and myself went up in the police boat to sound the depth of water, previous to our taking the cutters up the North Johnstone. We found the next suitable camp for tents about eleven miles up, and the shoalest soundings two fathoms, and at the camp seven fathoms, with lilies along both banks, and a stream of water 250 yards wide, with high banks and splendid soil. Mr. Hill says any man might come blindfolded and make a selection, all the land being equally good, and good water frontage along the whole distance. The site chosen for our next camp is at the junction of a small creek with the main stream, the angle formed being cleared of all rubbish and recently used by the blacks as a bora ground. We found two fine shields in the camp. I shot a moor hen and a new kind of fly-catcher.

October 10th.—Took the vessels up to Bora Camp. I went up ahead in the police boat and found a large mob of blacks collected to oppose us ; we dispersed them. The vessels arrived safely, and the camp was pitched. In the afternoon I again sent the troopers out, and went and found the blacks closing in on the camp, and dispersed them ; and during my watch at night they attempted to stalk the camp, but were frustrated ; and in the morning they came out below the camp and challenged us to come to them. We dispersed them.

October 11th.—We found tracks of a large mob of blacks where we heard them the night before. Mr. Dalrymple went up the river with five troopers ; I remained in camp with other troopers, anticipating an attack ; but in the afternoon I went out, but saw no fresh traces of blacks. Both returned at 3 p.m., having reached the head of navigation owing to rapids about four miles above Bora Camp.

October 12th.—Sub-Inspector Tompson, myself, and Mr. Hill, with five troopers, went up in the police boat about three miles above the rapids, and had to return, owing to more rapids. The stream, where we turned back, was 200 yards wide, shallow and rapid, with high banks, and the soil very rich.

October 13th.—Started at 5 a.m. to take the vessels back to Coquette Point ; arrived there at 4 p.m., and pitched the camp on the old site. The blacks were here ; we moved them on. Shot some weaver birds. The cutters arrived at 7 p.m.

October 14th.—Left Coquette Point at 8 a.m., and anchored off the South Frankland, where I shot enough Torres Strait pigeons to supply all hands, eight mallee hens, and we got a lot of cocoanuts. Pitched the camp on west side of the island.

October 15th.—Sailed at 4 a.m., and anchored off Rocky Island in Trinity Bay. I shot forty-three Torres Strait pigeons ; and found a beautiful new fern on this island. Blacks are numerous here.

October 16th.—Mr. Dalrymple and myself went in the police boat to sound into Trinity Harbor, about which there had been much speculation amongst us, I being the only one who had a bad opinion of it as an agricultural river, which turned out to be perfectly correct. We found nine feet of water on the bar at low water. The vessels sailed straight in and anchored inside. We found the harbor to be an immense mass of mangroves, intersected by saltwater channels varying in width from eighty to 200 yards, and forming the mangrove mass into innumerable islands. We returned to the junction of two main channels, and camped on board for the first time during the expedition.

October 17th.—Mr. Dalrymple, Hill, and myself went up in the police boat, and Sub-Inspector Tompson in the dingy up the main arm of the harbor to the head of navigation, and landed and went

through

through the mangroves, and found it to consit of poor granity sand ridges, timbered with pandanus, bloodwood, stunted tea-tree, and Moreton Bay ash, running off into tea-tree swamps. We saw several blacks in canoes with outriggers, but did not molest them, as they were inclined to leave us alone. We returned to the entrance, and pitched the camp on the north side of the entrance, near a native well, where there is a good supply of fresh water and permanent.

October 18th.—Sailed for Double Island at 10 a.m., and made Double Island, at 11·30 a.m., and pitched the camp on S.W. point ; no game here ; island very rocky and slaty ; no water.

October 19th.—Mr. Dalrymple very ill with fever and cold and a bad leg ; he fell across the hatchway, and thinks he has broken a rib. No service to-day. Full-dress parade.

October 20th.—I was ordered to take police boat and find a suitable place for watering, and to ascend coast range and see the back country. Mr. Hill accompanied Sub-Inspector Tompson in the dingy with us. When we landed I divided the troopers, and, taking four, I went along the south beach. I crossed a steep spur, and found water close to the beach, but brackish, and determined to find better. After going a little further I saw a mob of blacks coming towards us, yelling and brandishing spears poised on the wommera, each carrying a bundle of spears in the left hand. I saw at once they intended attacking us, and made preparations accordingly. We found the flesh and part of the skeletons of four men (blacks) whom they had eaten ; we found the cooked flesh stowed away in dilly-bags for food. The blacks here have splendid canoes made of solid cedar logs—dug-outs—with outriggers, and capable of carrying fifteen or twenty men ; the paddles resemble cricket-bats, and others like bakers' wooden shovels. We found plenty of cedar and kauri pine here, but the soil is very poor, with slaty shingle mixed through it.

October 21st.—All hands in camp ; Mr. Dalrymple very ill with fever and bad leg.

October 22nd.—Went on shore with police boat and dingy to water ; the surf was running very high, and we had great difficulty in filling up.

October 23rd.—Struck camp at 6 a.m. to start for the Endeavour ; anchored off Snapper Island, and remarked the entrance of a good-looking river in the mainland. Snapper Island is very pretty, but very little game on it ; I shot some Torres Strait pigeons, scrub hen, and a new sandpiper here.

October 24th.—Struck camp at 5 a.m. and made the Endeavour at 4 p.m. ; landed, and pitched camp close to the tree reported to have been marked C by Captain Cook ; during the night the "Flying Fish" sprung a leak, and damaged a great deal of our stores.

October 25th.—The s.s. "Leichhardt" came in at 10 a.m., much to our astonishment, and on board we met several old friends ; we got our mail, and altogether we had a busy day ; we were all pleased to hear of Mr. Nind and party's safe return to Cardwell.

October 26th.—Full dress parade ; no service.

October 27th.—Out shooting ; got a few pigeons and a deaf adder ; saw and got some fruit of the nonda tree, of Leichhardt and Kennedy celebrity ; found a tamarind tree and cotton tree.

October 28th.—Went up the Endeavour in police boat with Mr. Dalrymple ; the banks, where they are open, are composed of poor sandy soil, timbered with poplar gum, stunted tea-tree, Moreton Bay ash, and bloodwood ; saw flood marks ten feet over the banks in places ; we went up about eleven miles, to where a creek joins the main river from the southward, and landed on a small plain of about twenty-five acres of passably good soil. We then ascended a small hill on the east side of the creek, where we met Mr. MacMillan on the top, and, judging from the appearance of the range, I should not anticipate any difficulty in getting a good road through to the Palmer.

October 29th.—Started at 7 a.m. with Mr. Dalrymple and Captain Saunders and Tompson in the "Swift" steamer to explore the Annan and Esk. We found three feet of water on the bar at low water ; we went up about four miles ; the banks are miserable poor soil, the timber being principally poplar gum ; we returned to camp about 4 p.m. and found MacMillan had returned, reporting having been as far as main range, and found good road with plenty of water.

October 30th.—All hands, with the exception of crews of cutters, on board the "Leichhardt" at 4 p.m., to return to the Barnards. A blackfellow showed up about noon, and took Lieutenant Connor's flags, which he had erected on the point of a sandpit, about six hundred yards from the steamer. I told off two of my troopers—Jimmy and Sambo, belonging to the Cashmere detachment—to accompany Mr. MacMillan to the Palmer.

October 31st.—Anchored off the Three Islands ; went on shore and saw the process of curing bêche-de-mer—a most disgusting process.

November 1st.—Camped off the North Frankland ; Mr. Dalrymple informed me he was going on to Cardwell, giving me instructions to take command of the Expedition during his absence, and to explore a river I had noticed on my previous trip under Clump Point from our proposed camp on the South Barnard, and there to await his return.

November 2nd.—Arrived at South Barnard, and formed camp ; shot numbers of Torres Straits pigeon and scrub hens ; the steamer went on about noon.

November 3rd.—I took troopers and went over to mainland at 3 a.m. ; sounded into the Maria Inlet, and found the bar very shoal and banks inside ; found large log of pine on the beach, branded IN on the end ; found plenty of fresh water at the back of the beach ; the country is sandy, and timbered with bloodwood, plum, white apple, and tea-tree.

November 4th.—Went over to mainland, accompanied by Sub-Inspector Tompson and Mr. Hill to explore the Maria Inlet, so named because it was here the ill-fated captain and crew of the "Maria's" whaleboat were attacked and most of them brutally murdered by the blacks after abandoning their boat, which is now our police boat. The small range on the south side we named Sabine Range, after the officer of the "Basilisk," who recovered the boat and administered punishment to the savages for their horrid massacre of defenceless men. We went up for about six miles, and then there was a complete wall of mangroves, barring further progress ; we landed in two places and found the country at the back to be swamp and sand ridge ; we returned to the camp in the evening.

November 5th.—Went to the North Barnard to get some specimens of the Victoria rifle bird, and succeeded in getting six specimens, also numbers of Torres Straits pigeon, scrub hen ; returned to South Barnard on

November 6th.—The cutters arrived at 6·15 p.m., and reported having had fine weather the return trip. H.M.S. "Beagle" was in the Endeavour when the cutters left. The "Coquette" reported having seen

seen two large canoes coming in from the Barrier with twenty men in each, and as the cutter bore down towards them they paddled alongside of each other, and lashed themselves together, and prepared to fight, but the cutter did not molest them.

November 7th.—Started the "Coquette" to Cardwell, as per instructions from Mr. Dalrymple, after having taken her stores out; Mr. Hill sent specimens of botany in by her.

November 8th.—All hands cleaning arms and washing.

November 9th.—"Coquette" arrived from Cardwell with instructions from Mr. Dalrymple to send "Flying Fish" in, as he had chartered the schooner "Flirt" to complete expedition.

November 10th.—The "Flying Fish" started for Cardwell at 11 a.m., after having transhipped her stores into the "Coquette"; struck camp to remove to Dunk Island for watering; a heavy sea was running, and as the case containing the ammunition was being passed up from the boat to the cutter a sea struck the boat, and the case dropped between the ships' side and the boat and immediately sank; we could not recover it. As soon as I had formed the camp on Dunk Island I started for Cardwell in the police boat to report the loss to Mr. Dalrymple; I arrived at Cardwell at 11 p.m., and at daylight started for police camp, and succeeded in getting sufficient ammunition to complete expedition.

November 11th.—Went to Lower Herbert police camp.

November 12th.—Returned to Cardwell with ammunition.

November 13th.—"Bunyip" arrived; all ready on board the "Flirt" for a start **at daylight.**

November 14th.—Started in police boat, being towed by "Bunyip," for **camp on Dunk Island; arrived at 10 a.m.** ; the **"Flirt"** arrived at 7 p.m.

November 15th.—Filling up water on the "Flirt," and getting firewood on board.

November 16th.—Full dress parade; service at 11 a.m.

November 17th.—Sailed at 7.30 a.m.; fair wind; anchored off the North Frankland at 8 p.m.

November 18th.—Sailed at 7 a.m. for the Mulgrave River, which enters the sea immediately under Bellenden Kerr, and opposite the Frankland Islands; we entered the river in the police boat; we found four feet of water on the bar, and deep water inside; ascended the south branch, called the "Russell," about eight miles, and then returned to the schooner outside, and anchored off the South Frankland.

November 19th.—Sailed at 6 a.m. with land breeze; the wind failed us at 9 a.m., so we anchored off High Isle, the most northern of the Frankland Group; I went on shore with Mr. Hill and troopers; found two fine running streams of good water, one on the north side near a clump of pandanus, and the other in a small bay on the S.W. side; saw several whip snakes; shot scrub hen and Torres Strait pigeon; a large steamer passed us at 9.30 p.m., going south.

November 20th.—No wind; the s.s. "Bunyip" passed us going south, I went on board; no news of the Palmer; we stood into the Mulgrave, and anchored about three miles up, at the junction of the Mulgrave and Russell; we then took the police boat and ascended a tidal creek running up between the junction of the two rivers; it ran out in a marine plain under Bellenden Kerr; we returned to the ship at two p.m.; the blacks here are very numerous, but peaceable; they "cooey" to us occasionally; we went on shore on the north side and saw some very fine kauri pine, and catokidozamias fifty feet high; the Davidsonia plum tree also is very plentiful.

November 21st.—Ascended the Mulgrave about sixteen miles; five miles up we had fresh water; the mangroves extend about four miles up, and the banks are clothed with dense jungle, consisting of lawyers, palms, fern trees, pandanus, Moreton Bay chestnut, plane trees, figs, bananas, several Eugenias, Davidsonia plum, and tamarind trees; the banks are low in places, and subject to floods; the soil is very rich. I shot black duck, snipe, Torres Strait pigeon, moor hen, and saw king pigeon, scrub hen, and plenty of cockatoos; saw several lots of blacks, with canoes or dug-outs with outriggers, similar to the Trinity Bay ones mentioned previously; we fixed on a spur for the ascent of Bellenden Kerr; this river drains the north and east faces of Bellenden Kerr, and the country west of Walsh's Pyramid, one of the most remarkable mountains in the district.

November 22nd.—Went with troopers to look for watering place near the vessel, but could not find it in sufficient quantities.

November 23rd.—Service at 11 a.m.; weather fine and breezy.

November 24th.—Took the schooner up the Mulgrave to "Expedition Bend," and **took the boats** up and filled up with water; shot two alligators.

November 25th.—Hill, myself, and eight troopers started for the ascent of Bellenden Kerr; we left vessel at 8 a.m., with four days' rations each; we landed at Expedition Bend on the north side of small creek, and found the scrub very dense, and interwoven with lawyers and bamboo; at 12 noon we reached the base of the mountain, and crossed a fine stream of water sixty yards wide; the country between the river and base of range is all flooded; we filled our water-bags, and commenced the ascent; the leading spur is one dense mass of lawyers, bamboos, fern-trees, and vines, growing among large granite boulders; the trees are principally whitewood, Moreton Bay chestnut, she-pine, a new kind of kauri pine, several Eugenias; of birds, we saw Torres Straits pigeon, king-pigeon, scrub hen, pink-headed doves, king-parrots, three kinds of flycatcher, and rifle birds; we camped on top of the first shoulder; and the aneroid read 28° 78', and thermometer 68°, at 9 p.m.; heavy rain in the night.

November 26.—Started at 6 a.m., and after three hours' hard cutting through bamboo, lawyers and dwarf palms and fern-trees, we rose to a height of 2,100 feet, and saw some plains up the Mulgrave near Walsh's Pyramid, and plains up the Russell also; the spur we were on ran extremely narrow in places, with precipices on both sides, of which we could not see the bottom, our only footing being about eighteen inches wide for spaces of fifty yards at a time, and only a few small bushes to assist us in keeping our balance.

November 27th.—Started at 6 a.m.; aneroid read 26° 30', thermometer 68°; no water; we determined to reach the summit, and put ourselves on rations of water last night—half-a-pannikin for tea, and the same for breakfast; at noon we reached the centre top of Bellenden Kerr; heavy clouds; no view to be obtained, owing to the clouds being below us, where a heavy thunder-storm was raging; we sent up a big smoke, but the storm rose up to us, and everything was in semi-darkness; heavy rain set in; the aneroid read 24° 33', and thermometer 64°; everything, the whole distance up, showed signs of great drought, the mosses and lichens crumbling to pieces when touched; there were no flowers, and very little fruit, on any of the stunted trees and shrubs on the summit; Mr. Hill gathered specimens of all,

all, I think; we remained about an hour, and then commenced returning; the vegetation on the summit consisted of a small species of palm (*Keati* variety), fern-trees (*Alloophylla*) and stunted trees of various kinds; on the summit I saw only two birds, a kind of bower-bird; I shot them with my snider rifle, but spoiled them for specimens; the rain kept us company till 7 p.m., when we camped, having built ourselves waterproof palm gunyahs; Mr. Hill found here a very beautiful new fern-tree, also the wedding plant of Howe Island—an iris, called *Robinsonia*, after the present Governor of New South Wales; we also got a fine collection of small and beautiful ferns, and, to us a great treat, plenty of water.

November 28th.—Started at 6 a.m. for the schooner, and on the last shoulder I got a good view of the low country, and was enabled to get a round of bearings.

November 29th.—Very busy cleaning arms, and found that the new snider breech-action is not as good for wet weather as the old style.

November 30th.—Service at 11 o'clock; in the afternoon I took the boats up, to fill up with water, and returned on board at 7 p.m.

December 1st.—Explored the south branch, called the Russell, and found the mangroves to extend six miles up, intersected with patches of good land leading back to the extensive jungle at the back; the soil is very rich, but the banks are low, and subject to floods in places; there are two fine creeks coming from the Bellenden Kerr Ranges—the first about five miles up on the north side, which we called "Crinum Creek," from the quantities of that lily growing on its banks; it is a fresh-water creek; the other about three miles further up, on the same side, which we called "Olfersia Creek," from the great quantities of that fern on its banks.

December 2nd.—Started at 7·30 a.m., and arrived at the bar, but could not get out owing to head wind; Mr. Dalrymple sent me in shore with Mr. Hill and troopers to look for fresh water, and about a mile along the beach I found a fine stream of running water; I saw some blacks' gunyahs at the landing, which I had examined on a previous occasion, but one being much larger than the generality, I went to measure it, and found it to be 23 yards in circumference, and nearly circular; on going inside to measure the height, I found a splendid specimen of a mummy*—it was a woman, about 5 feet 6 inches high; she was squatted on her haunches, her hands clasping her face, and bound in the position by thin strips of lawyer-cane; the body was well preserved, and even the eyes were perfect; the ears, fingers, toes, and muscles, all showed as in a person dead from hunger; I imagine it had been tanned, as there was a quantity of scraped mangrove bark in the mouth, and the curing process had been completed by constantly subjecting to the smoke of fire in the gunyah; the mummy had been placed there in the interval between my two visits, with the idea of intimidating us, as the troopers were very frightened of it, and asked me not to take it on board, but I considered it too great a prize for the Museum to leave behind; we left some blankets and a tomahawk in the humpy where it was taken from, by order of Mr. Dalrymple. After lunch I went on shore, on the north side, to examine for water, and about three-quarters of a mile from the vessel we found a very fine lagoon, 400 yards long and 200 wide, of good water; returned to ship at 5 p.m., and attempted to get out, but the wind failed us, so we anchored inside.

December 3rd.—Started at 6 a.m., and crossed the bar all right, sighted a brigantine off the Franklands going south; after beating all day we got close to Fitzroy Island, and at 8 p.m. we were caught in a heavy squall, which lasted till 11 p.m., when we reached the anchorage off Fitzroy.

December 4th.—Watering ship; all hands washing; at 2 p.m. a ketch passed us, going south; saw fresh tracks of pigs in the scrub, but was too busy to try to get any.

December 5th.—Got under sail for Low Island at 8 a.m., but the wind failed us, and we were drifting about all night.

December 6th.—Got a breeze off the land at 4 a.m., and stood in for the opening marked in the chart near Snapper Island; the vessel anchored in three fathoms, and Mr. Dalrymple, Hill, and myself, went in the police boat, and found a small river which was called the "Mossman"; we went up about four miles, and found some rich jungle land; we then returned to the schooner, and stood up for the opening we had noticed on our previous visit to Snapper Island in the cutters; we went in the police boat, and succeeded in finding a good channel with six feet of water on the bar at low water; we then took the schooner in and anchored inside; saw plenty of blacks, but they seemed inclined to be friendly.

December 7th.—At 6 a.m., a canoe came off to us with eight men; we gave them shirts, blankets, &c.; they are a very miserable poverty-stricken looking lot of men, but have good dug-out canoes, with outriggers; we took the schooner about two miles up.

December 8th.—Took the vessel about one and a-half miles higher up, and then Mr. Dalrymple, Hill, myself, and troopers, went off in the police boat to examine the river, and found it to be a magnificent river, with rich jungle land on both banks, but traces of floods having broken over the banks in places; we went up about ten miles, when we landed, and I went on to the top a small range called the "Heights of Daguar"; they are a succession of fine open grassy hills of good soil; the extent of rich jungle land is very extensive, and Mr. Hill pronounces the soil to be first class; we found a new palm belonging to the cocoanut tribe.

December 9th.—Explored the south branch of this noble river, which was named the "Daintree," and found it to be a saltwater tidal inlet; we returned to the ship, and got under sail for the mouth, where we anchored.

December 10th.—The blacks came down at 6 a.m., to have a look at us, while others put off in a canoe, and made for Snapper Island. Mr. Dalrymple went in the police boat to sound the channel, after landing Hill, myself, and four troopers on the north side; we found it to be a narrow strip of sandy ground, backed by mangroves; I ascended Cape Kimberley for a look-out; we found a native well of good water under the cape at the first rocks approaching from the southward; we then went to examine the south side, and found a tract of good sound ridges, and good water in two native wells; we saw a camp of blacks, and stalked them; they were very frightened, but became friendly when we did not molest them; they gave us some shells and a wimmera, and we parted good friends; we sailed at 2·30 p.m., and saw a schooner anchored at the Low Islands; we sailed all night.

December 11th.—We made the South Franklands, where we anchored; I went on shore, and shot ten brace of Torres Strait pigeon, and a brace of scrub hen, several other good bags were made; we also got a lot of cocoanuts; we returned to ship at 6 p.m.

December

---

* Now in the Brisbane Museum.

47

December 12th.—Went off in police boat at daylight, and got a load of cocoanuts; saw a cutter going south; we sailed at 7 a.m. for the Johnstone, and anchored inside at 3 p.m.; when Hill and myself, in the police boat, ascended the South Johnstone, and landed about a mile above the first island on the east side, and cut through the jungle for three-fourths of a mile, where we took samples of the soil, and returned to the ship; shot an alligator alongside.

December 13th.—Went with Mr. Hill in the police boat to the junction of the South Johnstone, where we landed immediately opposite the junction on the north side of main stream; we cut through the jungle for about a mile; we took samples of the soil, and found one of the noblest fig-trees it is possible to imagine; it measured, three feet from the ground, one hundred and fifty feet nine inches in circumference; we then went down the river about a mile, and landed on the south side, and went back about a mile; we then ascended Nind's Creek, about two miles from the mouth of the river on the south side, and found it tapped a great extent of the rich jungle land on the Johnstone; we returned to the vessel at 6 p.m.

December 14th.—Service at 11 a.m.; the blacks yelling and going through the tragedy of murdering the "Maria's" crew. After service, I landed and found they had dug up the remains of one of them (I dispersed them); we filled up the watercasks in the afternoon.

December 15th.—Unable to get out to-day, owing to head wind, all hands on shore washing.

December 16th.—Heavy rains; Mr. Dalrymple, Hill, and myself, went up to Nind's Camp; returned to ship in the afternoon.

December 17th.—Heavy squalls all night, the wet season having set in in earnest; got under sail at 7 a.m.; got outside at 8 a.m., and beat up to Mourilyan Harbor.

December 18th.—Entered Mourilyan Harbor at daylight, and anchored off Camp Point; we then started in the police boat to examine the two creeks entering the harbor on either side of Ethel Hill; we went up the creek on the east side of the hill, about six miles, and found it headed close to Nind's Creek, in the Johnstone, making another navigable creek tapping the sugar lands of this district; we then returned and ascended the other, which was called the Arnit; we ascended the creek for about five miles, and camped at Ethel Hill for dinner, which Mr. Hill and I ascended, and on the top I went up a cinnamon tree and got a splendid view of the whole district.

December 19th.—Landed at Camp Point to fill up with water, and to enable Mr. Hill to get some botanical specimens; we also went to the top of Esmeralda Hill for Mr. Dalrymple to take some bearings.

December 20th.—We got outside at 10 a.m., and stood over to the South Barnard; saw a steamer going north, I went off with the police boat to meet her, but she would not stop or allow us to come near her, so I returned to the vessel, and then the steamer, having seen the vessel, which was hidden by the island previously, stood in and anchored alongside; the captain explained his not stopping for us, by having mistaken us for "Myall" blacks trying to cut them off; they had all their arms loaded ready to receive us; she proved to be the "Annie," of Adelaide, bound for Port Darwin; we landed and shot eighty-four head of Torres Strait pigeons.

December 21st.—We sailed at daylight and stood round Tam O'Shanter Point to examine the Hull, which proved to be only a tidal inlet.

December 22nd.—Sailed at 3 a.m. for Cardwell, and arrived there at 11 a.m.; I remained till 3 p.m., and then Mr. Dalrymple gave me permission to return to my district; consequently, I started in the police boat with my troopers, and arrived at the camp, December 23rd, at 5 p.m.

The health of the members of the Expedition throughout has been, on an average, good; but Mr. Dalrymple has been a great sufferer from the effects of a severe fall off a horse previous to starting, and an attack of fever; I thought it would have terminated fatally in the Mulgrave, but we were all delighted to see him recover before returning home.

I may mention, that the police boatman, John Perry, proved himself a good seaman, having sailed the boat all the way to the Endeavour, and always ready and willing to do any duty told off to him; we could not have had a better man for the boat.

The detachment of troopers were all that could be wished, and on no occasion had I to speak to any of them for neglect of duty, and they were always willing to do all they could; their health has been uniformly good throughout.

I have, &c.,

ROBERT JOHNSTONE,
Sub-Inspector Police.

The Commissioner of Police, Brisbane.

48

Botanic Garden,

Brisbane, 30th January, 1874.

Sir,

I have the honor to submit the accompanying report upon the nature of the country I had the opportunity of inspecting whilst along with the late expedition to the north-eastern coast. My present remarks apply almost entirely to the capability of the land for agriculture and settlement, leaving for another report a more direct reference to the botany of the region visited.

In presenting the following description of the different coastal rivers examined, I regret that it is not in my power to give more account of the back country intervening; to have made the description complete, it would have been necessary that the Expedition should have travelled by land. The primary object, however, being to explore the rivers, the work was done in boats; and it was not possible, even had there been time, to penetrate the mangrove swamps which line so great a proportion of the river banks and coasts of Northern Queensland. Of course, I cannot report upon what I did not see; but, judging from analogy, there must be a great deal of good land, besides that particularised below, back from the rivers and between the ranges in which they take their source, and the sea.

When leaving Brisbane to join the Expedition, I took with me a useful collection of **seeds and growing plants**, which I sowed and planted in suitable positions on the mainland and the islands. **A list** of these is given at the end of this Report, as well as memoranda of the samples of soil I obtained from different localities, and the shells I collected.

In a subsequent report, I shall describe the appearance and botany of the Bellenden Kerr Range, which is useless for settlement at present, when so much good land is available elsewhere, on account of the scrubby nature of the hills and the surrounding country from which they must be approached.

I have, &c.,

WALTER HILL.

The Honorable The Secretary for Public Lands, Queensland.

Dunk Island was the first place we visited, and we called at it a second time on our return. It is eight or nine miles in circumference, the centre being elevated, with a peak at either end. The island was carefully examined, and we found to contain about a thousand acres of first-class agricultural land, situated on the western and south-eastern side.

The great proportion of the soil is a very rich yellow loam, adapted for the cultivation of sugar, coffee, &c., &c. I may describe this land as consisting of scrub with belts of forest. The vegetation is composed of the genera *Hellenia, Musa, Calamus, Brunonia, Myristica, Wormia, Alstonia, Eucalyptus, Acacia,* &c., &c. It is well watered with small creeks of fresh water running through it here and there. There is abundance of timber for building purposes, and clay suitable for making bricks is also found. On the eastern side and north-east end of the island the land is for the most part covered with scrub, and is of too steep a nature to admit of cultivation being carried on.

I may remark that the largest and finest shade trees I have seen are growing on the border of the beach on the eastern side. They consist of *Calophyllum Inophyllum, L.; Terminalia melanocarpa, F.M.; Hernandia ovigera, L.; Eugenia grandis, F.M.,* &c., &c.; and form a fine avenue for the natural promenade of the beach. I trust that, should the Government part with the land on this island, a stipulation will be made that the trees will be saved.

After leaving Dunk Island, we proceeded to Moarilyan Harbor. On the south side of this opening the coast forms a steep range for a distance of about three miles. A similar range extends from the north entrance of the harbor for some miles. The land situated on the western slope of the southern range consists of a strong yellowish loam, well suited for the growth of tropical and semi-tropical products, but particularly for coffee and the different spice plants, cinnamon, nutmeg, clove, allspice, &c. The soil is equally well adapted for the sugar-cane, but the country being hilly, it will scarcely be used for that purpose whilst more level land is available. The ground is clothed with a dense mass of vegetation, consisting of the genera *Aleurites, Fitzgeraldia, Bruces, Aglais, Carapa, Buchanania, Seaxacarpus, Erioglossum, Cinnamomum, Myristica, Cordwelli, Archidendron,* &c., &c. The presence of these alone in the locality may be considered as an indication of first-class land.

There are springs of fresh water to be found close to the entrance to the harbor, and there is a fresh-water creek about a mile and a-half along the bottom of the range.

The Moresby Range, which is the one on the northern side, extends **to** the Johnstone River. The agricultural land on the western side varies from half-a-mile to a mile in breadth, and is of similar description, as regards both soil and vegetation, to the range on the southern side. Water is also found at the foot.

After entering the harbor and passing some low ground covered with a dense growth of mangroves, we came to Walter's Creek, which flows in from the right hand at about two miles from the foot of Moresby Range, to which it runs nearly parallel. We examined this creek for about five miles, where it became too narrow to admit the passage of the boat. About three miles up, on the left bank, a narrow belt of sound ground is seen, extending back to the Moresby Ranges. All the rest of the country on that side, up to the foot of the range, is composed of a mangrove swamp, from a mile to a mile and a-half in width. On the right bank of the creek, about four miles up, we found a narrow belt of scrub, which leads to the dividing ridge between the Rivers Johnstone and Walter's and the Armit Creek.

At the entrance to Walter's Creek, on the left hand going in, is Ethel Hill, some 150 feet in height, about a mile in length and half-a-mile in breadth. The soil is a strong loam of a dark yellow color, and of the very best description. It is covered with dense vegetation; but, although well adapted for cultivation, it forms such a fine building site that I think it ought to be reserved for that object.

Higher

49

Higher up the harbor, and three-quarters of a mile beyond the mouth of Walter's Creek, we found on the right hand, the entrance to Armit's Creek, and followed it up to the head of boat navigation, a distance of six miles. With the exception of Ethel Hill, which separates the mouths of the two creeks, the whole of the land on the left bank of the Armit is low, and nearly all covered with mangroves as far as the right bank of the Walter. On the right bank of Armit's Creek, about four miles up, we discovered a narrow piece of forest ground leading towards the high country to the westward, which is apparently the main dividing range. A mile further up is a patch of about 100 acres of scrub, suited for sugar cultivation.

The River Moresby, which is the principal affluent of the harbor, was examined for a distance of twelve or fourteen miles, when it became too narrow for the passage of the boat, although the water was deep enough. There were found only three patches of agricultural land, each having about a quarter of a mile of frontage to the river, and apparently isolated from one another by low marshy ground.

The soil in these places is of a fine quality, and adapted for sugar cultivation. The natural vegetation is composed of Colomas, Licistons, Cordwelli, &c., &c. From the head of navigation of the Moresby, as far as Moralba Hill, the right bank of the river and the same side of the harbor are lined with mangroves, which extend as far as could be seen inland from the bank.

We next proceeded to the Johnstone River, and anchored at Coquette Point, about a mile inside of the bar. On inspection of the country south of the mouth of the river, a fine sandy beach was found, and extending back from it, for about a mile in length and from 100 to 300 yards in breadth, a tract of land between the sea and the Moresby Range.

The soil is here, for the most part, of a sandy description, and scantily covered with Melaleuca, Eucalyptas, &c., &c., the remainder of the area being mangrove swamp. The range is well studded with Myristica, Cordwelli, Caparis, &c., &c., and from a mile south of the Johnstone forms the coast line. It is there covered with scrub vegetation, but it is too steep to admit of profitable cultivation at present. On the western side of the range the soil and vegetation, and of course the productive capabilities, are identical with what has already been described of this tract of elevated land on either side of Mourilyan Harbor.

On the north side of the mouth of the Johnstone there is a sandy beach up to Flying-fish Point, and behind the beach is a succession of gently rising hills, well covered with vegetation, and with abundance of fresh water. These eminences also possess the advantage of being within the full influence of the sea breeze, and would form an excellent site for villa residences when a township is established and the river becomes settled. I would suggest that the land should be reserved for this purpose, with the view of being cut up and sold when required.

From Coquette Point up to Nind's Creek, both sides of the river are covered with mangroves, which extend back as far as could be seen. From Nind's Creek up to the head of boat navigation, a distance of twelve or fourteen miles, the soil on both banks of the river, and for a mile inland, I ascertained to be the very best description, and may be described as consisting of very rich yellow and brown loams, adapted for the cultivation of sugar-cane. The extreme richness of the soil, and the evenness of the surface, render it not so suitable for the growth of the Coffee plant, spices, &c., &c.; indeed the natural vegetation would appear to indicate this. The genera are chiefly Musa, Colocasia, Costus, Helleaia, Aroads, Bombaus, Colocasia, Ficus, &c., &c., which are very abundant, and their presence alone may be considered as conclusive evidence of the exceeding fertility of the soil. The trees and shrubs lining the banks show marks in only a few places of the lower ground being overflowed in times of heavy floods. Five miles above Coquette Point the water is fresh and can be used for any purpose. I have described only the land within a mile from the river, as that was all that I had an opportunity of inspecting. I am convinced in my own mind, however, that the same description of soil will be found for a long way back, probably as far as the ranges, which appear to be some miles distant at the lower part of the river, but close in nearer towards its head.

From the mouth of the south branch to the head of navigation by boats, is a distance of about ten miles. Its banks are lined with Hibiscus, Aroads, Colocasia, &c., &c.; and only in one or two places were there indications of a portion of the land being covered in times of heavy floods. The soil, for a mile inland (which was as far as I could go), consists of strong yellow and brown loams, and densely covered with vegetation. The plants of the arboreal class belong to the genera Aletania, Cedrela, Oxonia, Sterculia, Cestanosperma, Nephelium, Caparis, Cordwelli, Eugenia, Archideadron, Fitzgeraldia, &c., &c. The undergrowth consists of Musa, Helleaia, Trudesentia, &c., &c. The presence of these trees, &c., &c., is a sufficient indication of the richness of the soil. The ground is also nearly all even in surface, and the fresh water supplied by this branch of the river is fit for any purpose.

At the head of navigation, we extended our examination inland for a distance of about two miles and a-half, to the top of Basilisk Range, which is the only elevation in the neighborhood that is not closely timbered. There are about fifty acres of open forest land along the top of the ridge, the trees consisting of Casuarina, Eucalyptus, Acacia, &c., which are of stunted growth, on account of the poor character of the soil, which is of a sandy nature. From the summit we had a splendid view of the surrounding country, which appeared to be, except in one or two places, a mass of dense vegetation.

Nind's Creek was examined for a distance of eight miles, which was as far as we could go, on account of the stream being too narrow for the passage of the boat. At the head of navigation the banks on either side were high, and well covered with vegetation. The country on both sides of the creek contained patches of scrub, alternating with marshes. On the right bank, the scrub, in one or two places, reached as far as the Moresby Range, thus affording a means of transit for settlers at the latter place, should the mangrove swamps be found to shut them out from communication with the river.

There are other apparently detached patches of scrub along Nind's Creek, varying from two hundred to five hundred yards in length, the intervals between lying too low for cultivation. The soil is not equal to that on the river, already described, nor is it so well covered with natural vegetation. Although the Musa, Helleaia, &c., are abundant, I would beg to suggest that the right bank of the river, from Nind's Creek to the south branch, and one mile up the latter, and on the left bank of the river, from opposite Nind's Creek to a quarter of a mile above Nind's Camp, be surveyed into farms of one hundred acres. From this, however, there might be reserved some four hundred acres, situated at the upper end, on the left bank, upon which land the large fig-tree mentioned in my telegraphic report was

6   found

found. By having small farms, the settlement of population would be ensured; whilst at the same time the soil is so rich that even a portion of the hundred acres would make a plantation profitable enough to encourage small capitalists to invest their money on the land. It would also be advisable that near the line on the south branch, recommended to be reserved, a road should be surveyed to the head of navigation of one of the streams which fall into Mourilyan Harbor. This would be found convenient, not only for the cultivators and others resident on the south branch, but also for those of the main river.

At Nind's Camp, which is situated at the junction of the south branch with the river, I would recommend that 640 acres be reserved, and surveyed in portions of 150 acres each, which could either be sold or let on lease. This position would be found a suitable one for the erection of mills for the use of the numerous planters who would settle in the neighborhood. In all the surveys suggested it would be of importance to make ample provision for roads, not only on account of the convenience to the settlers of such reservations, but also because they would have the result of materially increasing the effect of other precautions that might be taken to prevent the land from falling into the hands of mere speculators. It may also be stated that timber for building is found in large quantities and of good quality, the principal trees being Cedrela Toona, Rox; Aglaia elaeagnoidea, Benth; Oweaia Verrucosa, F.M.; Flindersia Bragleana, F.M.; Buchanania angustifolia, Rox; Alphitonia excelsa, Reiss; Harpullia Leichhardtii, F.M.; Sarcocephalus cordatus, Mig.; Cordwellia sublimis, F.M.; &c., &c.

The reserve of 400 acres which I have above suggested to be withheld from sale or selection would be a very suitable place for an experimental plantation for the benefit of cultivators of the sugar-cane, or of other tropical plants best grown on low land, or which might be propagated there, such as coffee and spice plants, &c., although they require higher ground for their subsequent successful cultivation. Reserves of 640 acres at the heads of navigation both of the main river and the south branch, might with advantage be made for the sites of future townships.

The next river north of the Johnstone is the Mulgrave, which at Cowrie Point, three miles inside of the bar, receives the waters of a south branch, and also of the Russell River. At the southern side of the entrance is a sandy beach a mile in length, and behind it sandy forest ground scantily covered with bloodwood (Eucalyptus corymbosa), &c., &c. From here to the banks of the south branch there is a mangrove swamp. At the southern end of the forest land and close to the beach there is a fine stream of running water, which comes from the range that begins here.

On the northern side of the entrance to the Mulgrave there is another beach two miles in length, at the back of which the land is mostly of a sandy character, and is sparsely covered with Eucalyptus, Melaleuca, Pandanus, &c., &c. About the middle of this tract there is a large lagoon of fresh water. Between the forest ground and the Russell the land is nearly all covered with mangroves, with the exception of about three acres near Cowrie Point. This spot is some three feet above salt-water mark, and is surrounded with mangroves. The soil is of a sandy description with a large admixture of decomposed vegetable matter. The principal trees are Dessnera robusta, R.B., sixty to eighty feet in height and three to four feet in diameter; Cordwelli sublimis, F.M.; Alstonia scholaris, R.B.; Elaeocarpus grandis, F.M., also of great size; and Catakitexaesis Hopei, W.H., upwards of sixty feet in height, with the trunk measuring seven feet in circumference three feet from the ground. This is the lowest situation in which I have found the latter tree. The highest elevation in which I have seen it was four thousand feet above the sea. It is the grandest of the Cycadæ.

From Cowrie Point the banks of the Russell are thickly lined with mangroves for the distance of a mile, after which they occur sparsely for another three miles or so, the remainder of the land being covered with Hibiscus, &c. Further on to the head of navigation, which is about sixteen miles from Cowrie Point, both banks are well covered with vegetation. The ranges approach near the river in some places, and large patches of mangrove swamp are found here and there.

The land suitable for sugar cultivation consists of brown and yellow loams of good quality. The principal trees, &c., are Cardwelli, Grevellia, Aleurites, Bambusa, Calamus, Musa, Hellenia, &c., &c. The ranges are also well covered with trees, &c., &c., the vegetation being similar to that found on the Moresby Range, and the soil of the same character. Several fresh-water creeks and springs were found along the river and at the foot of the ranges. The river water can be used at about eight miles from Cowrie Point.

The length of the south branch to the head of boat navigation is about fourteen miles, for four or five miles of which distance the banks are lined with mangroves. The land suitable for cultivation of the sugar-cane between the ranges and the river is mostly confined to narrow belts, and in many places are separated by long intervals of low swampy ground.

The agricultural land referred to appeared to be above flood mark, and was well studded with Calamus, Cordwelli, &c. The banana and wild ginger plants, which are plentiful on the Russell River, are not so frequently met with on this branch. The soil is similar in character to that of the Russell. The ranges on each side resemble the Moresby Range, as regards soil and vegetation. We followed up two creeks that run into the left bank,—the first about four miles from Cowrie Point. The land on both was unsuitable for cultivation, being low and swampy.

We also traced up a creek opposite Cowrie Point for about six miles, which led to a low marine plain covered with Pandanus aquaticus, F.M. There are several fresh-water creeks in different parts of the tract of country just described, and the water in the river is drinkable about eight miles from the Point. Timber of the best description for building purposes is plentiful, and also clay suitable for making bricks.

I would beg to suggest that the land I have described, on which the Cowrie pines are situated might be made a timber reserve; also, a strip of land on the right bank of the river, on which the same trees grow. Should this not be done, a very valuable description of timber will be exterminated from the district.

The next place we visited was Trinity Inlet, which extends inland for some seven or eight miles. On either side of the entrance is a sandy beach, which at a short distance is closed in by the coast range. The inlet had the appearance at first of a river much broader than the Brisbane. We expected to make some useful discoveries here from the promising look of the surrounding country, but met with complete disappointment. The inlet and its shores form a basin or amphitheatre walled in by mountain scenery of a grand and picturesque nature, the spurs in some places sweeping down towards the water. A lower grassy

grassy hill **near** the head of the inlet had a most promising look, but although we spent two days in endeavoring **to find** a watercourse that would lead us to the high ground, our progress was everywhere stopped by a universal mangrove swamp. Beyond the open water of the inlet, the low-lying country is covered with mangroves, and is penetrated by a perfect network of creeks and branches, none of which took us to firm ground. The mangroves here, *Burguiera Rheedi (Blume), Burguiera gymorrhiza (Lam.)*, &c., are of unusually large size, and may some day be turned to commercial account, as the bark is much sought after in China for tanning purposes.

To the north of Trinity Inlet is the Mossman River, which was examined for a distance of five miles. On either side of the entrance there is a sandy beach stretching along the coast for about a mile; and behind the beach, on the south side, there is a narrow belt of sandy forest ground leading to some grassy ridges of easy ascent, which appeared to be thinly covered with *Eucalypti*. For about a mile up the river the land is generally low, and lined with mangroves; but from that distance to the farthest point to which we proceeded there are several patches of high ground showing **no** signs of being flooded, and closely covered with vegetation. The soil is a strong yellow loam; the trees consisting of *Alstonia*, *Cedrela, Cardwellii, Castanospermum, Brassia, Architendron*, &c., &c. Beyond the **distance** of five miles to which our exploration extended the country had the appearance of a fine valley, **reaching a** long distance into the ranges, densely clothed with trees and shrubs.

Farther to the north than the Mossman is the Daintree, to all appearance the finest river that **we** had entered. We anchored about two miles inside the bar. On the south side a sandy beach extends for some two **or three** miles, behind which there is a strip of sandy forest ground **from a** hundred to three hundred yards in width, sparsely covered with *Casuarina*, &c., &c. **Fresh water was found** in native wells in several places, where the *Melaleuca leucodendron, L.*, grow in clumps. On the northern side there is also a fine beach, extending to the foot of a rocky range, which terminates at the coast. Here, also, there is a narrow belt of sandy forest ground at the back of the beach, having a few trees—*Eucalyptus*, *Pandanus, Acacia*, &c.; and a good spring of fresh water flows from under the rocks at the back of the beach. We rowed up the river for a distance of sixteen miles from the estuary, and found the banks, for about six miles, low, and almost uninterruptedly fringed with mangroves. The land immediately adjoining is in many places still lower, and being naturally swampy, and subject to be periodically inundated with brackish water, it is chiefly remarkable for the exuberance of its marine vegetation. Continuing up the river, in the next tract of country, the mangrove is replaced by the *Hibiscus*, and the land is densely covered with tropical vegetation, consisting chiefly of the genera *Mimusops, Wrightea, Cardus, Cocos, Carica*, with numerous other trees and shrubs, &c., peculiar to these districts. The description of the trees and their luxuriant growth would alone testify to the natural richness of the soil. The extent of the land suitable for sugar-cane between the river and the ranges varies from a quarter of a mile to several miles in breadth. At the farthest point we reached, we landed on the right bank and examined a fine open forest ridge, about a mile inland, and some three hundred feet in height. It was thinly studded with *Eucalypti* and *Acacia*, and the soil covered with grasses, of which the *Anthistiria ciliata*, *R.B.*, (Kangaroo grass), was the most abundant. From the summit a most magnificent scene presented itself; an extensive valley opened out before us, stretching far to the north, the east, and the west.

The banks of the main river, with branches of less size flowing into it, could be traced to far in the distance, bordered with dense vegetation extending for miles back from their banks. We also observed many low grassy ridges thinly clad with trees, and elevated plains or plateaus were seen about the heads of some of the watercourses. Near this, our farthest point, the Palmer Range approaches near the river, and appears to join on to another range more to the westward. The latter appears to offer an easier means of ingress to the Palmer River than any other place we had seen. From what I saw of the Daintree River, and of its upper valley just referred to, it appeared to me to be well adapted to support a large population, and to afford openings for prosecuting a greater variety of industrial pursuits than any other of these coast rivers. There is abundance of land for the cultivation of the sugar-cane and of other tropical productions; there is also a large quantity of pastoral land, and I feel convinced that from this river will be found the best and easiest route to the newly discovered mineral region beyond the ranges from which its head waters flow.

Timber suitable for building purposes is almost everywhere to be obtained, and stone, as well as clay for bricks, &c., is easily procurable.

The next river which we explored was the Annan, which we followed up for a distance of three miles or so from its mouth. On the northern side, a sandy beach extends to nearly the foot of Mount Cook, and the southern head is formed by the termination of a range which projects into the sea. After entering the river, the banks are in some places thinly fringed with mangroves, and on the right bank there is a narrow belt of low land well covered with vegetation.

At the northern side of the entrance the land is high, apparently everywhere above flood mark. It is a sandy forest ground scantily covered with trees, the more predominant of which are *Eucalypti*, *Grevillia*, &c. The grasses are *Anthistiria ciliata, R.B.*; *Chloris divaricata, R.B.*; *Cenchrus Australis*, *R.B.*, &c., &c., which also grow somewhat sparsely. Beyond the highest point we reached, the country had every appearance (as well as it could be judged of from a distance) of containing a better description of land than that of the lower part of the river.

The Endeavour River was examined for a distance of ten miles from its mouth. On the northern side the land is too low to admit of being successfully cultivated, and both banks are fringed with mangroves. On the south side is Mount Cook, a steep elevation covered with trees, which grow down to the edge of the rocky shore. Farther up, extending for about five miles in length, and back inland to the ridge that divides the Annan from the Endeavour, the soil is of a poor sandy nature, the vegetation consisting of *Eucalyptus, Parkinsonia*, &c., &c. The only good ground found during that distance was a narrow belt on each side of a creek about a mile and a-half from the wharves, which I would beg to suggest should be reserved, along with the creek, for water supply. There is also a plain of some forty acres in extent, and a narrow belt of scrub situated on the right bank at the highest point to which we ascended. The soil in each case is of good quality, and the vegetation indicates that **the** land can be cultivated with success. East of the plain we ascended a small open forest ridge, about a hundred feet or so in height, where there is a fine view of the surrounding country. We could trace the course of the river for a considerable distance up, the ground through which it flowed being low and not of an inviting description.

On

On our return trip, we examined the Maria Inlet, which is about fourteen miles north of Tam O'Shanter's Point. On the northern side is a fine sandy beach extending some two or three miles, immediately behind which there is a narrow belt about two hundred feet in breadth. The soil is of a sandy nature, with a little admixture of vegetable matter. The trees consisted of *Calophyllum Inophyllum*, L.; *Terminalis melanocarpa*, F.M.; *Hernanda Origera*, L.; *Eugenia grandis*, F.M., &c., &c. They grow so regularly that they have the appearance of being planted, and give to the place the aspect of a well laid out park. At Dunk Island, the *Calophyllum* surpasses all other trees for shade, but here the *Eugenia* takes the lead. The trunk is taller and stouter than any that can be compared with it, its branches extend a greater distance, the foliage is much closer, the flowers give a better effect at a distance, and it bears a fruit which is often used as a relish. In the study and practice of my profession I have visited the Royal Parks, and the most celebrated of those belonging to the nobility and landed gentry of the mother country; but the natural groves of Maria Inlet, to my taste, produced a far more pleasing effect than any work of the landscape gardener's art which I have seen. At the south side there is a small sandy beach, and behind it some elevated ground well covered with trees and herbage. We traced the inlet up for a distance of ten miles, which was as far as we could go, and to our great disappointment we stopped in the midst of an extensive mangrove swamp. The banks of the inlet generally are low and composed of a sandy soil, the vegetation consisting chiefly of *Eucalyptus*, *Barringtonia*, *Wormia*, *Casuarina*, &c., &c.

The next and concluding river of the mainland which we examined was the Hull, which is south of Tam O'Shanter's Point. We followed it up for a distance of twelve miles from the mouth, and found the banks, for the most part, extremely low, and almost uninterruptedly lined with mangroves. On the left bank there are four narrow belts of forest and scrub land, at intervals of two or three miles apart, extending from the ridge to within a few yards of the water, thus affording a means of communication between the back country and the rivers, whilst everywhere else there is an impassable swamp. There is some open forest, and also dense scrub land, lying between the river and the coast, which is well adapted for the cultivation of sugar-cane, coffee, &c., &c.

In addition to Dunk Island, above described, several other islands were inspected, the more important being Fitzroy, No. 4; Frankland; North and South Barnard; and the largest of Brook's Groupe. Fitzroy Island rises to a considerable height; it is about five miles in circumference, and thinly wooded, with the exception of the banks of two or three streams between narrow gullies on the western side, which fall into the sea near a small bay, where the vessels visiting the island anchor. The forest trees are principally *Eucalyptus*, *Tristania*, *Casuarina*, &c., &c. The grasses were *Anthistiria ciliata*, *Cynodon polydactylon*, R.B.; *Leptaspis Bankii*, R.B.; &c., &c. The scrub vegetation consist of *Alstonia*, *Minusops*, *Gardenia*, *Cryptocarya*, &c., &c. The soil is of fair quality, but the greater portion of it is better adapted for grazing than agriculture. Some eleven years ago I visited this island, and was much struck by the fine appearance of the shade trees, particularly *Calophyllum inophyllum*, &c., &c., and which, in former times, had been highly spoken of to me by the captains of vessels calling at the islands. These trees have all been cut down, and no traces of them are to be found. But this is not all the wanton injury that has been perpetrated, for the many handsome tree-palms (*Livistonia inermis*) which used to adorn the lightly-clad forest ridges, all have been destroyed, with one exception. Frankland Island, No. 4, we found to be surrounded by a rocky shore, with the exception of a low sandy spot about three acres in extent, surrounded with a coral beach. The higher portion was thickly clad with *Myristica*, *Cedela*, *Dysoxylon*, *Aglaia*, *Geijera*, &c., and the lower part with *Hibiscus*, *Orcidpium*, *Aristolochia*, &c., &c. On the extreme end of the island we found two clumps of cocoanut-trees, extending for about fifty yards inland, but within reach of the sea spray. They were twenty-eight in number; thirteen of them were bearing, and the others will bear in the course of two or three years. Three or four of them were about fifty feet in height. The trunks, in some cases, were much cut; and two trees had been felled, no doubt for the purpose of obtaining the nuts. It is to be regretted that there is no means of preserving cocoanut-trees from destruction in this way, for there is no necessity for cutting them down in order to obtain the fruit.

The Barnard Islands are surrounded with a rocky shore, with the exception of a small tract of sandy ground on the western side of the South Island, and a small coral beach on the north-western side of the north island. We found fresh water on both. The higher ground is well covered with *Myristica*, *Gyrocarpus*, *Cryptocarya*, *Tismania*, &c.; whilst the trees and shrubs on the margin of the lower ground consist of *Premna*, *Eucarpus*, *Ceathium*, *Leves*, &c., &c.

Brook's Island is situated about twenty miles south of Cardwell; it is about half-a-mile in length, and a quarter of a mile in breadth. With the exception of a narrow patch of coral beach on the north-western side, the shore is rocky. It is well studded with trees and shrubs, amongst which are *Premna acutanista*, R.B.; *Vitex globrata*, R.B.; *Clerodendron lanceolatum*, F.M.; *Diospyros rugossis*, R.B.; *Securilila serices*, R.B., &c., &c. The soil consists of a sandy loam with decomposed vegetable matter, but of no great depth. Fresh water was found, but it was not plentiful. The *Megapodius Tumulus* (a description of scrub turkey) and five species of pigeons were seen, together with several other kinds of birds.

In my opinion it would be expedient to reserve some of these islands for acclimatisation purposes. For instance, Fitzroy Island would be very suitable for such animals as Angora goats, the different varieties of the deer tribe, &c., &c., whilst Brook's Island would find food and good shelter for game birds that it might be considered advisable to introduce on the main land. I purchased in Brisbane a pair of Guinea fowls, and Mr. Sheridan, the Police Magistrate at Cardwell, who displayed a great interest in introducing and distributing plants and animals to be acclimatized, has also added to the stock (two females), and put them on shore along with the pair I took on Brook's Island.

SAMPLES OF SOILS.

Banks of the Moresby River, creeks, and ranges	...		...	...	7 samples.	
,,	Johnstone	,,	,,	...	...	10 ,,
,,	Mulgrave and Russell		...	...	5 ,,
,,	Mossman	...	...	...	...	1 ,,
,,	Daintree	...	...	...	...	2 ,,
,,	Endeavour	...	...	...	...	1 ,,
,,	Hull	...	...	...	...	2 ,,
,,	Fitzroy Island	...	...	...	...	1 ,,

SEEDS

53

SEEDS AND PLANTS SOWN AND PLANTED ON THE MAIN LAND AND THE ISLANDS.

Oryza Sativa	...	The rice plant.
Andropogon Sorghum	...	Guinea corn.
Setaria Italica	...	Indian millet.
Fagopyrum esculentum	...	Buckwheat.
Panicum junceitorum	...	Guinea grass.
Panicum spectabile	...	Angola grass.
Bromus Schraderi	...	Prairie grass.
Cardaminum officinale, R.B.	...	Watercress.
Arachis hypogæa	...	Ground nut.
Eriobotrya Japonica	...	Loquat.
Anona squamosa	...	Sweet sop.
Anona Chermolia	...	Chermoyer.
Anona reticulata	...	Custard apple.
Mangifera Indica	...	Mango.
Persia gratissima	...	Alligator pear.
Diospyros Kaki	...	Chinese date plum.
Artocarpus incisa	...	Breadfruit.

Artocarpus integrifolia	...	Jack fruit.
Nephelium Longan	...	Longan.
Coffea Arabica	...	Coffee.
Theobroma Cacao	...	Cocoa.
Myristica Moscata	...	Nutmeg.
Cinnamomum Zeylanicum	...	Cinnamon.
Caryophyllus aromaticus	...	Clove.
Piper nigrum	...	Black pepper.
Zingiber officinalis	...	Ginger.
Vanilla aromatica	...	Vanilla.
Manihot utilissima	...	Brazilian arrowroot.
Manihot Janipha	...	Brazilian tapioca.
Maranta arundinacea	...	West India arrowroot.

6 varieties of pine-apples.
6 varieties of mulberry.
3 varieties of sweet potatoes.
12 varieties of American vines.

SHELLS OF THE NORTH-EAST COAST EXPEDITION, COLLECTED BY W. HILL.

Cypraea Tigris	...	...	...	5	Bulla	3
„ arabica	...	...	...	11	Venus	9
„ carneola	...	...	...	1	Mytilus	3
„ Vitellus	...	...	...	0	Mitra (dead)	4
„ annulus	...	...	...	16	Dentatorera	6
„ small worn	...	...	...	13	Neritina Martoniana	20
Telina	...	...	...	5	Auricula	23
Vitrina (3 broken)	...	...	...	9	Cassianella	1
Helix	...	...	...	95	Venus	3
Helix McGilleray	...	...	...	2	Conus (alive)	2
Chama	...	...	...	1	„ (dead)	12
Littorina	...	...	...	41	Cerithium	3
Natica	...	...	...	2	Strombus	3
Neritina	...	...	...	22	Trochus	10
Cypraea (young)	...	...	...	1	Turbo	15
Nassa	...	...	...	5	Scarabaeus	90
Nerita	...	...	...	5	Madiola	3
Purpura	...	...	...	9	Melania	12
Haliotis	...	...	...	1	Pterocera	3

By Authority: JAMES C. BEAL, Government Printer, William street, Brisbane.

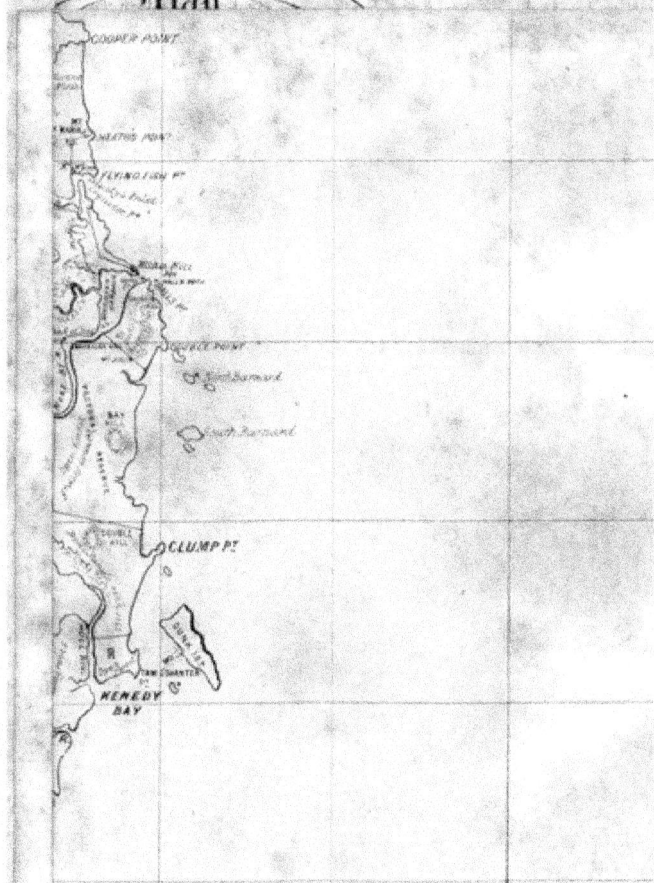

Map

Map
of
EXPLORATIONS & DISCOVERIES
by
G. Elphinstone Dalrymple
commanding
THE QUEENSLAND NORTH EAST COAST EXPEDITION.
1873.
BETWEEN CARDWELL & CAPE BEDFORD.

www.ingramcontent.com/pod-product-compliance
Lightning Source LLC
Chambersburg PA
CBHW022036080426
42733CB00007B/860